FREE Test Taking Tips DVD Offer

To help us better serve you, we have developed a Test Taking Tips DVD that we would like to give you for FREE. **This DVD covers world-class test taking tips that you can use to be even more successful when you are taking your test.**

All that we ask is that you email us your feedback about your study guide. Please let us know what you thought about it – whether that is good, bad or indifferent.

To get your **FREE Test Taking Tips DVD**, email freedvd@studyguideteam.com with "FREE DVD" in the subject line and the following information in the body of the email:

> a. The title of your study guide.
>
> b. Your product rating on a scale of 1-5, with 5 being the highest rating.
>
> c. Your feedback about the study guide. What did you think of it?
>
> d. Your full name and shipping address to send your free DVD.

If you have any questions or concerns, please don't hesitate to contact us at freedvd@studyguideteam.com.

Thanks again!

Six Sigma Green Belt Study Guide

Six Sigma Green Belt Exam Prep Team

Table of Contents

Quick Overview

As you draw closer to taking your exam, effective preparation becomes more and more important. Thankfully, you have this study guide to help you get ready. Use this guide to help keep your studying on track and refer to it often.

This study guide contains several key sections that will help you be successful on your exam. The guide contains tips for what you should do the night before and the day of the test. Also included are test-taking tips. Knowing the right information is not always enough. Many well-prepared test takers struggle with exams. These tips will help equip you to accurately read, assess, and answer test questions.

A large part of the guide is devoted to showing you what content to expect on the exam and to helping you better understand that content. Near the end of this guide is a practice test so that you can see how well you have grasped the content. Then, answer explanations are provided so that you can understand why you missed certain questions.

Don't try to cram the night before you take your exam. This is not a wise strategy for a few reasons. First, your retention of the information will be low. Your time would be better used by reviewing information you already know rather than trying to learn a lot of new information. Second, you will likely become stressed as you try to gain a large amount of knowledge in a short amount of time. Third, you will be depriving yourself of sleep. So be sure to go to bed at a reasonable time the night before. Being well-rested helps you focus and remain calm.

Be sure to eat a substantial breakfast the morning of the exam. If you are taking the exam in the afternoon, be sure to have a good lunch as well. Being hungry is distracting and can make it difficult to focus. You have hopefully spent lots of time preparing for the exam. Don't let an empty stomach get in the way of success!

When travelling to the testing center, leave earlier than needed. That way, you have a buffer in case you experience any delays. This will help you remain calm and will keep you from missing your appointment time at the testing center.

Be sure to pace yourself during the exam. Don't try to rush through the exam. There is no need to risk performing poorly on the exam just so you can leave the testing center early. Allow yourself to use all of the allotted time if needed.

Remain positive while taking the exam even if you feel like you are performing poorly. Thinking about the content you should have mastered will not help you perform better on the exam.

Once the exam is complete, take some time to relax. Even if you feel that you need to take the exam again, you will be well served by some down time before you begin studying again. It's often easier to convince yourself to study if you know that it will come with a reward!

Test-Taking Strategies

1. Predicting the Answer

When you feel confident in your preparation for a multiple-choice test, try predicting the answer before reading the answer choices. This is especially useful on questions that test objective factual knowledge or that ask you to fill in a blank. By predicting the answer before reading the available choices, you eliminate the possibility that you will be distracted or led astray by an incorrect answer choice. You will feel more confident in your selection if you read the question, predict the answer, and then find your prediction among the answer choices. After using this strategy, be sure to still read all of the answer choices carefully and completely. If you feel unprepared, you should not attempt to predict the answers. This would be a waste of time and an opportunity for your mind to wander in the wrong direction.

2. Reading the Whole Question

Too often, test takers scan a multiple-choice question, recognize a few familiar words, and immediately jump to the answer choices. Test authors are aware of this common impatience, and they will sometimes prey upon it. For instance, a test author might subtly turn the question into a negative, or he or she might redirect the focus of the question right at the end. The only way to avoid falling into these traps is to read the entirety of the question carefully before reading the answer choices.

3. Looking for Wrong Answers

Long and complicated multiple-choice questions can be intimidating. One way to simplify a difficult multiple-choice question is to eliminate all of the answer choices that are clearly wrong. In most sets of answers, there will be at least one selection that can be dismissed right away. If the test is administered on paper, the test taker could draw a line through it to indicate that it may be ignored; otherwise, the test taker will have to perform this operation mentally or on scratch paper. In either case, once the obviously incorrect answers have been eliminated, the remaining choices may be considered. Sometimes identifying the clearly wrong answers will give the test taker some information about the correct answer. For instance, if one of the remaining answer choices is a direct opposite of one of the eliminated answer choices, it may well be the correct answer. The opposite of obviously wrong is obviously right! Of course, this is not always the case. Some answers are obviously incorrect simply because they are irrelevant to the question being asked. Still, identifying and eliminating some incorrect answer choices is a good way to simplify a multiple-choice question.

4. Don't Overanalyze

Anxious test takers often overanalyze questions. When you are nervous, your brain will often run wild, causing you to make associations and discover clues that don't actually exist. If you feel that this may be a problem for you, do whatever you can to slow down during the test. Try taking a deep breath or counting to ten. As you read and consider the question, restrict yourself to the particular words used by the author. Avoid thought tangents about what the author *really* meant, or what he or she was *trying* to say. The only things that matter on a multiple-choice test are the words that are actually in the question. You must avoid reading too much into a multiple-choice question, or supposing that the writer meant something other than what he or she wrote.

5. No Need for Panic

It is wise to learn as many strategies as possible before taking a multiple-choice test, but it is likely that you will come across a few questions for which you simply don't know the answer. In this situation, avoid panicking. Because most multiple-choice tests include dozens of questions, the relative value of a single wrong answer is small. Moreover, your failure on one question has no effect on your success elsewhere on the test. As much as possible, you should compartmentalize each question on a multiple-choice test. In other words, you should not allow your feelings about one question to affect your success on the others. When you find a question that you either don't understand or don't know how to answer, just take a deep breath and do your best. Read the entire question slowly and carefully. Try rephrasing the question a couple of different ways. Then, read all of the answer choices carefully. After eliminating obviously wrong answers, make a selection and move on to the next question.

6. Confusing Answer Choices

When working on a difficult multiple-choice question, there may be a tendency to focus on the answer choices that are the easiest to understand. Many people, whether consciously or not, gravitate to the answer choices that require the least concentration, knowledge, and memory. This is a mistake. When you come across an answer choice that is confusing, you should give it extra attention. A question might be confusing because you do not know the subject matter to which it refers. If this is the case, don't eliminate the answer before you have affirmatively settled on another. When you come across an answer choice of this type, set it aside as you look at the remaining choices. If you can confidently assert that one of the other choices is correct, you can leave the confusing answer aside. Otherwise, you will need to take a moment to try to better understand the confusing answer choice. Rephrasing is one way to tease out the sense of a confusing answer choice.

7. Your First Instinct

Many people struggle with multiple-choice tests because they overthink the questions. If you have studied sufficiently for the test, you should be prepared to trust your first instinct once you have carefully and completely read the question and all of the answer choices. There is a great deal of research suggesting that the mind can come to the correct conclusion very quickly once it has obtained all of the relevant information. At times, it may seem to you as if your intuition is working faster even than your reasoning mind. This may in fact be true. The knowledge you obtain while studying may be retrieved from your subconscious before you have a chance to work out the associations that support it. Verify your instinct by working out the reasons that it should be trusted.

8. Key Words

Many test takers struggle with multiple-choice questions because they have poor reading comprehension skills. Quickly reading and understanding a multiple-choice question requires a mixture of skill and experience. To help with this, try jotting down a few key words and phrases on a piece of scrap paper. Doing this concentrates the process of reading and forces the mind to weigh the relative importance of the question's parts. In selecting words and phrases to write down, the test taker thinks about the question more deeply and carefully. This is especially true for multiple-choice questions that are preceded by a long prompt.

9. Subtle Negatives

One of the oldest tricks in the multiple-choice test writer's book is to subtly reverse the meaning of a question with a word like *not* or *except*. If you are not paying attention to each word in the question, you can easily be led astray by this trick. For instance, a common question format is, "Which of the following is…?" Obviously, if the question instead is, "Which of the following is not…?," then the answer will be quite different. Even worse, the test makers are aware of the potential for this mistake and will include one answer choice that would be correct if the question were not negated or reversed. A test taker who misses the reversal will find what he or she believes to be a correct answer and will be so confident that he or she will fail to reread the question and discover the original error. The only way to avoid this is to practice a wide variety of multiple-choice questions and to pay close attention to each and every word.

10. Reading Every Answer Choice

It may seem obvious, but you should always read every one of the answer choices! Too many test takers fall into the habit of scanning the question and assuming that they understand the question because they recognize a few key words. From there, they pick the first answer choice that answers the question they believe they have read. Test takers who read all of the answer choices might discover that one of the latter answer choices is actually *more* correct. Moreover, reading all of the answer choices can remind you of facts related to the question that can help you arrive at the correct answer. Sometimes, a misstatement or incorrect detail in one of the latter answer choices will trigger your memory of the subject and will enable you to find the right answer. Failing to read all of the answer choices is like not reading all of the items on a restaurant menu: you might miss out on the perfect choice.

11. Spot the Hedges

One of the keys to success on multiple-choice tests is paying close attention to every word. This is never more true than with words like *almost, most, some,* and *sometimes.* These words are called "hedges" because they indicate that a statement is not totally true or not true in every place and time. An absolute statement will contain no hedges, but in many subjects, like literature and history, the answers are not always straightforward or absolute. There are always exceptions to the rules in these subjects. For this reason, you should favor those multiple-choice questions that contain hedging language. The presence of qualifying words indicates that the author is taking special care with his or her words, which is certainly important when composing the right answer. After all, there are many ways to be wrong, but there is only one way to be right! For this reason, it is wise to avoid answers that are absolute when taking a multiple-choice test. An absolute answer is one that says things are either all one way or all another. They often include words like *every, always, best,* and *never.* If you are taking a multiple-choice test in a subject that doesn't lend itself to absolute answers, be on your guard if you see any of these words.

12. Long Answers

In many subject areas, the answers are not simple. As already mentioned, the right answer often requires hedges. Another common feature of the answers to a complex or subjective question are qualifying clauses, which are groups of words that subtly modify the meaning of the sentence. If the question or answer choice describes a rule to which there are exceptions or the subject matter is complicated, ambiguous, or confusing, the correct answer will require many words in order to be expressed clearly and accurately. In essence, you should not be deterred by answer choices that seem excessively long. Oftentimes, the author of the text will not be able to write the correct answer without offering some qualifications and modifications. Your job is to read the answer choices thoroughly and completely and to select the one that most accurately and precisely answers the question.

13. Restating to Understand

Sometimes, a question on a multiple-choice test is difficult not because of what it asks but because of how it is written. If this is the case, restate the question or answer choice in different words. This process serves a couple of important purposes. First, it forces you to concentrate on the core of the question. In order to rephrase the question accurately, you have to understand it well. Rephrasing the question will concentrate your mind on the key words and ideas. Second, it will present the information to your mind in a fresh way. This process may trigger your memory and render some useful scrap of information picked up while studying.

14. True Statements

Sometimes an answer choice will be true in itself, but it does not answer the question. This is one of the main reasons why it is essential to read the question carefully and completely before proceeding to the answer choices. Too often, test takers skip ahead to the answer choices and look for true statements. Having found one of these, they are content to select it without reference to the question above. Obviously, this provides an easy way for test makers to play tricks. The savvy test taker will always read the entire question before turning to the answer choices. Then, having settled on a correct answer choice, he or she will refer to the original question and ensure that the selected answer is relevant. The mistake of choosing a correct-but-irrelevant answer choice is especially common on questions related to specific pieces of objective knowledge, like historical or scientific facts. A prepared test taker will have a wealth of factual knowledge at his or her disposal, and should not be careless in its application.

15. No Patterns

One of the more dangerous ideas that circulates about multiple-choice tests is that the correct answers tend to fall into patterns. These erroneous ideas range from a belief that B and C are the most common right answers, to the idea that an unprepared test-taker should answer "A-B-A-C-A-D-A-B-A." It cannot be emphasized enough that pattern-seeking of this type is exactly the WRONG way to approach a multiple-choice test. To begin with, it is highly unlikely that the test maker will plot the correct answers according to some predetermined pattern. The questions are scrambled and delivered in a random order. Furthermore, even if the test maker was following a pattern in the assignation of correct answers, there is no reason why the test taker would know which pattern he or she was using. Any attempt to discern a pattern in the answer choices is a waste of time and a distraction from the real work of taking the test. A test taker would be much better served by extra preparation before the test than by reliance on a pattern in the answers.

FREE DVD OFFER

Don't forget that doing well on your exam includes both understanding the test content and understanding how to use what you know to do well on the test. We offer a completely FREE Test Taking Tips DVD that covers world class test taking tips that you can use to be even more successful when you are taking your test.

All that we ask is that you email us your feedback about your study guide. To get your **FREE Test Taking Tips DVD**, email freedvd@studyguideteam.com with "FREE DVD" in the subject line and the following information in the body of the email:

- The title of your study guide.
- Your product rating on a scale of 1-5, with 5 being the highest rating.
- Your feedback about the study guide. What did you think of it?
- Your full name and shipping address to send your free DVD.

Introduction to the Six Sigma Exam

Function of the Test

The Six Sigma Green Belt exam is part of the American Society for Quality's (ASQ's) Six Sigma Green Belt certification process, intended to serve as a signifier of excellence in quality and quality improvement. ASQ also says that Green Belt certification results in job promotions, salary increases, and added professional opportunities. Green Belts spend time on process improvement teams and operate in support of or under the supervision of Six Sigma Black Belts. Accordingly, individuals taking the Six Sigma Green Belt exam must have three years of full-time, paid employment working within the Six Sigma Green Belt Body of Knowledge.

The Six Sigma Green Belt exam is primarily taken by test-takers in the United States, but it is offered in testing centers worldwide. It is offered in English and Spanish at all testing locations, and in Mandarin at testing locations in China.

Test Administration

The Six Sigma Green Belt exam costs $288 for ASQ members and $438 for non-members. $70 of the fee is a non-refundable application fee. Test takers who fail the exam may retake the test at the retake rate. A retake attempt must be made within two years of the previous failed attempt; otherwise, the test taker must submit a new application and pay the full certification fee.

The test is typically administered by computer at Prometric testing centers, and only during six specific testing windows during the year. Windows last a few weeks and are spaced a couple of months apart. There are also special location exams offered from time to time, but most test takers take the standard, computer-based exam at Prometric. Within the testing windows, the test is typically available any day that the center is open for business.

Test Format

The Six Sigma Green Belt test consists of 110 multiple-choice questions (10 of which are experimental and not scored) and is administered over four-and-one-half hours. The examination is open book, and test takers are allowed to use any reference materials they bring with them to the exam that meet certain specific ASQ rules. Calculators are built-in to the computer-based testing software, and test takers are also allowed to use personal calculators provided they appear on an approved list.

Here's a look at the sections of the exam:

Topic	Questions	Description
Overview	13	Organizational goals and principles
Define Phase	23	Project identification; project management; business results; team dynamics
Measure Phase	23	Process analysis; probability and statistics; collecting data
Analyze Phase	15	Exploratory data analysis; Hypothesis testing
Improve Phase	15	Design of experiments; root cause analysis
Control Phase	11	Statistical process control; control plan

Scoring

A panel of experts examines each question and determines whether it will provide an appropriate assessment of the test taker. The panel also determines a passing score for the exam. The raw score is calculated based off of the total number of correct answers, and there is no penalty for incorrect answers. The raw score is then scaled to a scale of a total possible 750 points. A score of 550 is required to pass. Test takers do not receive a specific score; instead, the test is only reported pass or fail.

Overview

Six Sigma and Organizational Goals

Value of Six Sigma

The name *Six Sigma* was derived from the concept that there are six standard deviations between a customer's specification limit and the mean of a process. Six Sigma is centered on the idea that any process variation can be reduced using data collection, statistical tools, and sustained process monitoring. Six Sigma's ultimate goal is to correct a process so it's near perfect, generally allowing for no more than 3.4 defects per million opportunities. Organizations implement the Six Sigma methodology to increase profit and shareholder value and to reduce waste. In addition, Six Sigma practitioners hold belt titles that relate to their level of experience (i.e., Champion, Yellow/Green Belt, Brown/Black Belt, and Master Black Belt).

Quality Pioneers

Dr. Joseph M. Juran was one of the leading figures in the total quality management industry. The *Pareto Principle* (named after Italian economist Vilfredo Pareto) was one of his key ideas. When Juran applied this principle to his work, he identified that 80 percent of process issues were the result of 20 percent of process defects. This was commonly known as "the 80/20 rule." In addition, Juran was known for an improvement cycle known as the *Juran Trilogy* that is comprised of quality planning, quality improvement, and quality control. His quality planning roadmap provided a detailed approach to the activities associated with these three processes.

Quality Planning
- Identify customers and their needs
- Develop products to meet those needs
- Create processes that produce those products

Quality Improvement
- Create annual quality improvement monitoring
- Identify specific processes that need improvemnt
- Establish an improvement team

Quality Control
- Evaluate quality performance
- Compare actual quality to goals

Dr. W. Edwards Deming was another leader in the quality movement. He believed that a company could increase its market share and productivity while decreasing expenses by focusing on quality improvement. Deming was best known for his *14 Points for Management*, which applied to any size and type of business. These points served as a guide about what to change, although they didn't necessarily provide a step-by-step process of how to implement the recommended changes. The 14 Points were:

1. Create a constant purpose toward improvement in products and services.
2. Adopt the new philosophy.
3. Stop depending on inspections to achieve quality.
4. Strive to use a single supplier for any one item to minimize the total cost.
5. Improve constantly and forever on every process.
6. Utilize on-the-job training for employees.
7. Implement leadership.
8. Eliminate fear.
9. Break down barriers between departments and staff members.
10. Get rid of unclear slogans and targets for employees.
11. Remove numerical goals and quotas.
12. Remove barriers to pride of workmanship, as well as annual rating or merit systems.
13. Implement education and self-improvement programs for all staff.
14. Ensure it's understood that transformation is everyone's job.

Along with Juran and Deming, *Dr. Walter A. Shewhart* was another pioneer of the quality movement. Shewhart was known for developing *control charts*, which were tools for tracking process variation. He identified categories of variation known as *assignable-cause* and *chance-cause* (also referred to as *special-cause* and *common-cause*). A control chart can help catch variation early in the process, and also determine whether it's a special-cause or common-cause variation. Shewhart was also known for the *Plan-Do-Check-Act (PDCA)* cycle. This was an ongoing evaluation of procedures and managerial policies that led to continuous improvement. Four stages made up this cycle. The first stage involved *planning or identifying* the change or improvement that's needed. The next stage was *doing*, which focused on implementing the change. *Checking* was the third step, which involved measuring the process or outcome. *Acting* was the final stage that took place if the final results didn't turn out as expected or desired.

Dr. Kaoru Ishikawa was a proponent of taking quality improvement one step further to include the customer service component. His model aimed to provide consumers with excellent customer service after making a purchase from a company. Ishikawa was best known for his *fishbone diagram* (or *cause-and-effect diagram*). This tool helped stakeholders brainstorm a problem's possible causes and then organize them by categories to tailor a solution.

Organizational Goals and Six Sigma Projects

The goals that a company plans to achieve are further defined by measurable *objectives*. A company's *strategy* is its action plan for achieving those objectives. Ideally, a company's strategy, objectives, and Six Sigma initiatives should be closely aligned to promote an overall, continuous improvement culture. A company's objectives can increase the importance and effectiveness of Six Sigma projects, and Six Sigma professionals can work to ensure that the company's strategy is executed. For example, if a company's objective is to increase customer satisfaction by 10 percent, then a Six Sigma *voice of the customer (VOC)* initiative will become a top priority since it's directly related to attaining the customer satisfaction objective. As part of executing the company's strategy in this example, the Six Sigma project team may create customer surveys, gather customer data, and work with focus groups. Therefore, Six Sigma professionals can increase their value to the company by selecting projects related to the most important objectives. In addition, Six Sigma professionals can take on leadership roles throughout projects by practicing ongoing communications with leaders and employees and by showing staff how to execute strategies while providing them with solid feedback regarding process inputs and outputs.

Organizational Drivers and Metrics

The Six Sigma methodology can only deliver results successfully when it's aligned properly with a company's goals. This is best achieved by forming a team of key stakeholders throughout the organization (i.e., people invested in the process, ranging from upper management to actual workers carrying out the process) who can ensure that the implementation of Six Sigma projects is both effective and efficient in achieving organizational goals.

There are several key business drivers that initiate and benefit from well-designed Six Sigma projects. *Customer loyalty resulting from customer satisfaction* is a long-standing measure of a company's success. Six Sigma projects that aim to improve customer satisfaction do so by uncovering customers' requirements, reducing mistakes, increasing product or service quality, and continuing to design innovative products or services. *Improved supply chain management* can also be the focus of Six Sigma projects. Since having no more than 3.4 defects per one million opportunities is the overall goal of Six Sigma, lowering a company's number of suppliers is one way to reduce the risk of defects. Additionally, staying in constant communication with suppliers is crucial for a company, particularly if any supplier changes are planned that could affect the company's processes. Six Sigma projects can have a goal of *reducing inventory* since maintaining inventory requires capital from the company. Companies can also detect and repair defects in smaller product batches without creating slowdowns to the production cycle. *Cost efficiency* is yet another focus of Six Sigma projects, as manufacturing processes are restructured using lean methods. Finally, Six Sigma projects can have a goal of *reducing cycle times*, as manufacturing processes are restructured to eliminate waste and produce products faster.

The best *project metrics* are direct, meaningful, and simple. The metrics should reflect the needs of the customer as well as the company's business goals. Once the problem statement is understood, the project team performs a brainstorming exercise to determine the metrics that lead to increased performance. Upper management then reviews the metrics with the team to ensure they're aligned with the business goals.

The *balanced scorecard* is another approach to ensure that a Six Sigma project meets both the company's goals and the customer's needs when choosing the metrics for a project. The metrics displayed on a balanced scorecard span four perspectives: financial, customer, internal business processes, and employee learning and growth. The scorecard contains metrics that are financial and non-financial in nature, as well as measurements that are taken prior to the start of an event (leading) and those taken after the close of an event (lagging).

The *financial perspective* addresses the financial objectives that must be accomplished for the Six Sigma project to be deemed successful. Examples of scorecard metrics are: inventory levels, activity-based costing, cost of poor quality, and overall project savings.

The *customer perspective* looks at the customer objectives that must be met. Examples of scorecard metrics are: on-time delivery, customer satisfaction, and product quality.

The *internal business processes perspective* addresses the Six Sigma project by examining the processes that require modification or improvement to achieve the customer objectives. Examples of scorecard metrics are: cycle time, number of hours of rework, supplier quality, number of defects, and volume shipped.

The *employee learning and growth perspective* looks at how team members must learn and innovate to achieve the project's goals. Examples of scorecard metrics are: quality of training, total number of individuals trained in Six Sigma methodology, utilization of Six Sigma tools, effectiveness of meetings, and project schedule vs. actual date.

The project team typically holds a brainstorming session to determine the scorecard metrics. However, the project team must ensure that these metrics demonstrate a clear balance between the measurements taken before the start of an event (leading) and those taken after the close of an event (lagging), while also maintaining a relatively equal number of leading and lagging metrics.

As the Six Sigma project progresses, the balanced scorecard metrics are labeled as follows and reported on in meetings:

- *Red*: Results are below target and require immediate attention.
- *Yellow*: Results are within a tolerance interval below target and need to be monitored.
- *Green*: Results are at or above target.

These colors of the scorecard metrics alert Six Sigma Master Black Belts and Black Belts to project areas that require immediate attention. Metrics in red must be addressed in a timely manner to prevent other areas from being adversely affected by poor performance. For example, a metric that's marked as red in the internal business processes perspective (e.g., a manufacturing bottleneck that leads to a longer cycle time) can result in a metric turning to yellow or red in the customer perspective (e.g., lowered customer satisfaction ratings) if not addressed quickly. The balanced scorecard approach serves as a powerful communication tool for all members of the company.

Lean Principles in the Organization

Lean Concepts

Lean is sometimes referred to as "Lean Speed" or "Lean Methods." The goal of lean is to improve customer loyalty and product quality by reducing waste. This is accomplished by examining business processes to uncover and eliminate steps that either don't add value or are non-essential, which ultimately results in streamlined production. Lean is a way of thinking that can be applied to any organization, not just manufacturing companies. Lean methodology can be incorporated into Six Sigma project methodology when a company is working to improve an existing process, and increased efficiency or process speed is the focus of that improvement. When combined, the approaches of eliminating waste (lean) and increasing quality (Six Sigma) go hand in hand.

A lean concept known as the *Theory of Constraints* focuses on profit improvement by identifying and managing constraints. The premise behind this theory is that every company has at least one constraint that's holding it back from attaining more of what it wants, which is usually profit. An example of a common constraint is a bottleneck in the manufacturing process or in the market demand. The Theory of Constraints is an ongoing process that identifies and manages constraints, which leads to increased profits.

A *change agent* can guide staff through a five-step process to implement the Theory of Constraints within an organization. The first step is identifying a constraint in the system. Next is deciding how to best exploit the constraint. An example of these two steps might be determining how a company can reduce the downtime of a bottleneck in a manufacturing process without applying a costly upgrade.

Subordinating everything else takes place in the third step, which means other system components are adjusted to allow the constraint to operate most effectively. The system is also reassessed to ensure a constraint doesn't appear in another area. If steps two and three have been unsuccessful, then everything possible is done to eliminate the constraint (even major system changes). Step four involves elevating the constraint. The final step is taking the first step in the process again to ensure the overall state of the system is unchanged and experiencing no new constraints.

In addition, there are three measures used to increase profits through the Theory of Constraints: operating expense, throughput, and inventory. *Operating expense* is an expense that's not directly associated with a company's production, but rather with a company's daily activities (e.g., payroll, rent, and depreciation). *Throughput* is the rate at which a product or service is created and delivered to a customer, generating money for the company. Inventory is the part of a company's assets that is or will be ready to sell, so it's money that's tied up within a company. Ultimately, the goal is to minimize operating expense and inventory while maximizing throughput using the Theory of Constraints.

Jim Womack and *Daniel Jones* were the thought leaders in *lean management* who developed five principles of *lean thinking* to help companies guide the continuous improvement process. *Value* is the first principle of lean thinking. Customers are willing to pay a certain price for a product or service based on the associated value they place on it. Therefore, the lean philosophy places great importance on understanding the problems customers are trying to solve by purchasing a particular product or service and what drives its value. By understanding the price customers will pay for specific service offerings and product features, the focus can be placed on reducing cost and waste so the product and/or service can be delivered at the exact price the customer wants, while still making a profit for the company.

Creating a *value stream* is the second principle of lean thinking. It's important for companies to map out the specific actions (including materials, processes, and steps) that are required to bring a product or service either from new idea to launch or from order placement to customer delivery and final payment. This allows companies to visualize the entire process, making it easier to identify value-added activities, activities that don't add value but can't be eliminated (due to current system limitations), time delays, and waste (opportunities for improvement). Value stream mapping software can be very helpful to organizations during this step in the process.

The third principle of lean thinking is *flow and pull*. Lean organizations strive to increase the flow of products and services through the value stream based on the pull of customer demand. Companies practicing lean management strive to eliminate their work-in-progress inventory and produce products or services based on customer needs. This requires constant monitoring of the flow of the value stream and communication between various steps in the manufacturing process. Any step in the value stream that results in a customer waiting interrupts the flow and leads to decreased value. Therefore, it's essential that companies monitor all steps of the production and delivery flow.

Empowerment is the fourth principle of lean thinking. To provide the most value to the customer and eliminate waste from the process, management should give employees (such as shop floor and line workers) the information and authority to take the necessary actions at the right time, as needed. However, for this to be truly effective, staff must be well trained in their own processes and in lean methodology, have a clear line of sight to the company's strategies and goals, and be accountable for their actions.

The fifth principle of lean thinking is *perfection*. Companies that practice lean management continuously strive toward perfection by working toward the goals of zero defects and zero waste. Management should continue to keep employees informed about changing customer requirements, while staff should focus on making daily improvements in their work processes.

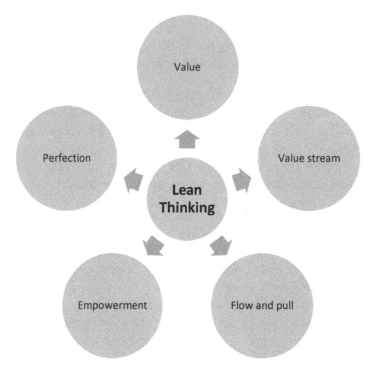

Value Stream Mapping

Value stream mapping is a visual means to identify and analyze a specific business process within a company. Once the decision is made on what to map out, the entire process used to create a particular product or service is examined, and each step is assigned a value. The value stream map ultimately reveals value-added steps or limitations in the process, such as excessive inventory or delays. In addition, by representing a process diagrammatically, employees are more clearly able to understand each other's work and associated issues.

Value stream mapping is best completed as a team exercise. The team should have members from the process areas that are being mapped, and they should be guided by an individual with previous experience in value stream map development. An overarching objective for completing the value stream map process (e.g., improving quality or decreasing lead times) must be decided on and agreed to by every team member before beginning the exercise.

Then the outer limits of the map from which the supply chain would start and end must be decided on. For example, if the value stream map is slated to flow from supplier to customer, then the raw materials (or the name of the company from which raw the materials are purchased) would serve as the starting point, and the final customer (or company name if the final consumer is a business) would serve as the end point. Next, all of the steps (or operations that take place for the product or service) are added in proper order between the start and end points as the team walks through the process. Additionally, *information flows* are added to the value stream map. These are the ways customers interact with the company (and how frequently) to order the product or service, how customer communications are sent to suppliers, and how customer requirements are translated into business processes to ensure the end products or services meet their specifications.

To ensure successful performance at every step in the process, the team collects data on relevant measures (e.g., inventory, cycle time, shifts worked, and number of employees) that are recorded as *data boxes* on the value stream map. *Inventory counts* are also added to the map.

To provide further information on inventory lead times and total process times, a *time line* is added to the map. To determine the total lead time, the inventory used at each step and the daily demand are used to calculate the amount of inventory in stock in days. This number is added to the top of the timeline. Then the *cycle time* for producing one product or service is added in the lower section, which is added to obtain the total processing time. This creates the *current state value stream map* and is the team's first trial of the value stream mapping process.

The team then takes time to analyze, reflect on, and share the current state value stream map with all stakeholders as their next step of the value stream mapping process. The value stream map's data boxes and timeline divulge information about problems within the particular process that need to be addressed, such as long cycle times and rework. There are eight types of waste that can be revealed by the current state value stream map:

- Errors that must be corrected at a later date (such as subsequent repairs) are a form of waste known as *defects*.

- Excessive inventory that loses value as it takes up space is another form of waste. Instead, it's better for a company to keep only a limited safety stock on hand.

- Employees who don't use their skills in the right place or in the best way at some point during the process are a form of waste, since employees are an integral part of a lean organization.

- Taking too many steps to produce a product or service is wasteful, since it requires more time, labor, and money to do so. This type of waste is known as *over-processing*.

- The incurred costs of time and money when there are wasted movements in the steps to produce a product or service. For example, an employee who needs to frequently access files stored on a different floor than their immediate work area.

- *Overproduction* that leads to excess inventory is a form of waste.

- Waiting is a form of waste. For example, an employee who must wait on instructions from another individual before carrying out their next activity.

- Any inefficient flow of an element that's needed in the process (such as a document or a material) creates a waste known as *transport*. This can occur from poor layouts or routing on warehouse or production floors.

The team works to develop cost-effective solutions that address the root causes of the problems in the current process. They also work to create a *future state value stream map* that details the best version of the process to try and reach the ideal state for the process.

The team's third review of their value steam map focuses on implementing improvements. It's important for the team to share the future state value stream map with all of the stakeholders in to gain their buy-in prior to implementation. Upon approval, all associated procedures and training materials are updated to reflect the changes in the process. The next step is to ensure that all affected employees are trained on the new procedures prior to implementation. Finally, the new process changes are implemented, and those changes with the greatest benefit are implemented first. It's important for the team to leave enough time between the implementation of each change to determine the resulting benefit.

The team's final review of the value stream map deals with ensuring that the process improvements are sustained. It's important for the team to monitor and, if necessary, reinforce the stakeholders' compliance to the newly implemented procedures. Any new staff that comes on board should be trained to adhere to the newly implemented procedures. Additionally, *key performance indicators (KPIs)* should be established to measure ongoing performance of the process. Ultimately, change will be validated by using the KPIs in conjunction with the baseline metrics of the current state process.

Design for Six Sigma (DFSS) Methodologies

Road Maps for DFSS

DMAIC is the most well-known and frequently used project methodology for a company working to improve an existing process. The methodology can be used on a process that's not performing as expected or not living up to customer specifications. DMAIC is an acronym for its five steps: *define, measure, analyze, improve,* and *control*. In the first step, the problem being addressed is defined. The next step involves measuring the problem and the associated process from which it was produced. Analyzing data to uncover the root cause of opportunities and defects takes place in the third step. Next, solutions are researched to improve the process and to fix and prevent future problems. In the final step, improvement solutions are executed and controlled to keep the process on track.

Design for Six Sigma (DFSS) is an approach that companies take when they need to create or redesign a product or process from the ground up to meet Six Sigma quality levels.

DMADV is an acronym for the most popular DFSS methodology that also consists of five steps: *define, measure, analyze, design,* and *verify*. In the first step, the problem to be addressed is defined. The next step involves measuring the customer's specifications. Analyzing the process to meet the customer's specifications is the third step. Next, designing a process to meet the customer's specifications is detailed. In the final step, the design's performance and ability to meet customer specifications is verified.

IDOV (Identify, Design, Optimize, and Verify) is another type of DFSS methodology. The first phase deals with accurately identifying the requirements for the new product or service through the *voice of the customer (VOC)* process. This data is collected through such methods as interviews with customers, surveys, complaint logs, or focus groups. The team and associated team charter are typically developed during this phase, as well as the *critical to quality (CTQ) factors*. A design concept is formulated in the design phase, along with identifying various design parameters and possible risks through the use of simulations tools. Procurement and manufacturing plans are also created during this phase. Appropriate business processes are chosen based on the CTQ factors from the identify phase. During the optimize phase, the existing design is optimized, alternative design elements are developed (as needed), and the performance capabilities of business processes are predicted. In the last phase of the process, the design is tested and validated, and any final changes to the business process are made.

Basic Failure Mode and Effects Analysis (FMEA)

Failure Mode and Effects Analysis (FMEA) is an approach used to identify all the possible ways that a design, assembly, or manufacturing process, service, or product can fail. FMEA also tries to identify the associated consequences of such failures. These failures are given prioritization based on their ease of detection, the seriousness of their consequences, and the frequency with which they occur. Beginning with the highest priority failures, the goal of FMEA is to eliminate or reduce them.

It's fitting to use FMEA when a product, service, or process is being designed or redesigned, or when an existing product, service, or process is being applied in a new manner. In addition, FMEA can be helpful when analyzing the failures of an existing product, service, or process, or before control plans are developed for a modified or new process. FMEA can also be beneficial when improvement goals are outlined for an existing product, service, or process.

FMEA typically begins with a cross-functional team of employees (i.e., individuals from customer service, design, quality, sales, manufacturing, purchasing, and testing) who are knowledgeable about the product, service, or process and the customers' needs. Then the team identifies the scope of the FMEA. Next, the team discusses the scope's function and add it to the FMEA form. For example, they may ask themselves what the purpose of the design, service, or process is and what their customers are expecting from it. The team then considers all the ways that failures can occur (*potential failure modes* or *PFMs*) and add them to the FMEA form. For each of the potential failure modes, the participants identify the associated consequences and list them in the FMEA form. Next, the team members rate the *severity (S)* of each consequence (or effect) on a scale of one to ten (where ten is catastrophic) and add those ratings to the FMEA form. Severity estimates how severe a customer or end user perceives a failure's effect to be. The root causes for each of the failure modes are discussed and listed on the FMEA form. Next, the team members determine the probability of each possible cause of failure that occurs during the life of the scope. These *occurrence ratings (O)* are also on a scale of one to ten (where ten is inevitable) and are added to the FMEA form. The next step in the process involves participants identifying the current process controls for each cause that are in place to prevent failures from affecting customers. Each process control is then assigned a *detection rating (D)* to demonstrate if it successfully detects either the cause or its failure mode after they occur but before the customer is affected. The *detection ratings (D)* are also on a scale of one to ten (where ten means there's no existing control) and are added to the FMEA form. Detection is sometimes referred to as "effectiveness" and refers to how well the controls perform to prevent or detect the cause or failure mode before the failure reaches the customer. The *risk priority number (RPN)* is then calculated by multiplying together the *severity (S)*, the *occurrence (O)*, and the *detection (D)*. RPN can range from 1 to 1000 (with 1 as the absolute best). The *criticality* is calculated by multiplying together the severity (S) and the occurrence (O). The RPN and the criticality can assist with ranking potential failures in the order they should be tackled. Finally, the team recommends actions to lower the severity or occurrence (such as process or design changes) and notes the individual(s) responsible and associated target completion dates.

It's important to note that, as a general rule, a failure mode with an effect resulting in a severity of nine or more has top priority, since severity is given the most weight when assessing risk. The combination of severity and occurrence is considered next, since this represents criticality.

Design FMEA and Process FMEA

An application of FMEA that's targeted for product design is known as *Design Failure Mode Effects Analysis (DFMEA)*. DFMEA is useful for uncovering potential failures with a product that can lead to shortened product life, product malfunctions, or safety issues during product use. DFMEA starts at the earliest stage of the design process, when design concepts are in the exploration phase of thinking through all scenarios of the design failing when functioning in the real world. A document is created and maintained that records the design's key functions and any potential failure modes and their causes. Then the team attempts to reduce the potential causes of the failure modes by applying various countermeasures. The main tool used throughout this process is a *DFMEA matrix*.

The design team that's typically used for DFMEA is led by a responsible design engineer. The cross-functional team members consist of a test engineer/technician, a marketing/product manager, a reliability/quality engineer, a field service engineer, and an employee from materials management/purchasing.

The *Process Failure Mode Effects Analysis (PFMEA)* is another application of FMEA. It is directed toward processes within a business unit or organization, and it analyzes failure modes associated with those processes. PFMEA is useful for uncovering potential failures that can lead to customer dissatisfaction, environmental or safety hazards, and process unreliability.

During a PFMEA, a document is created that exists throughout a product's lifecycle. Each process step is evaluated, and a score between one and ten is assigned to the steps based on four variables. The first variable is *severity*, which deals with the failure mode's impact on the overall process and the associated safety concern (where a score of one represents the least concern to safety and a score of ten represents the highest concern to safety). The second variable is *occurrence*, which deals with the failure's chance of happening (where a score of one means the lowest chance of occurrence and a score of ten means the highest chance of occurrence). The third variable is *detection*, which deals with a failure's chance of being detected (where a score of one means a failure will most certainly be detected and a score of ten means a failure will most likely not be detected). The last variable is the *risk priority number (RPN)*, which is calculated by multiplying the three rankings of severity, occurrence, and detection together for a *relative risk rating*. The value of the RPN falls between 1 and 1000, and the higher the RPN value the higher the risk. A corrective action is required for any RPN value that's higher than 80.

The process team typically used for PFMEA is led by a responsible manufacturing engineer. The cross-functional team members consist of a design engineer, a tooling engineer, a maintenance technician, a materials management/purchasing employee, a quality/reliability engineer, and responsible operators. During the course of the PFMEA, the team leadership changes to a process engineer who also served on the DFMEA team.

Practice Questions

1. Which Six Sigma quality leader is known for the *80/20 rule*, where 20 percent of the defects ultimately lead to 80 percent of the problems?
    a. Dr. W. Edwards Deming
    b. Dr. Walter A. Shewhart
    c. Dr. Joseph M. Juran
    d. Dr. Kaoru Ishikawa

2. Which Six Sigma quality leader is known for his *14 Points for Management* that serves as a guide about what to change?
    a. Dr. Kaoru Ishikawa
    b. Dr. Joseph M. Juran
    c. Dr. Walter A. Shewhart
    d. Dr. W. Edwards Deming

3. What diagram is used to brainstorm all possible causes of a problem in order to sort ideas into categories that ultimately lead to a solution?
    a. Plan-Do-Check-Act (PDCA) cycle
    b. Fishbone diagram
    c. Quality planning road map
    d. Value stream map

4. Which category is *NOT* one of the perspectives that metrics span across on a balanced scorecard?
    a. Environmental
    b. Financial
    c. Customer
    d. Employee learning and growth

5. What's the goal of the *Theory of Constraints*?
    a. Improve customer loyalty
    b. Increase employee satisfaction
    c. Reduce waste
    d. Increase profits

6. Which is *NOT* one of the five principles of lean thinking?
    a. Empowerment
    b. Flow and pull
    c. Employee satisfaction
    d. Perfection

7. Which of the following is a visual means to identify and analyze a specific business process within a company?
    a. Value stream mapping
    b. Ishikawa/fishbone diagram
    c. Failure Mode and Effects Analysis (FMEA)
    d. Design for Six Sigma (DFSS)

8. For a company working to improve an existing process, what's the most well-known and frequently used project methodology?
    a. Design for Six Sigma (DFSS)
    b. Identify, Design, Optimize, and Verify (IDOV)
    c. Define, Measure, Analyze, Improve, and Control (DMAIC)
    d. Failure Mode and Effects Analysis (FMEA)

9. Which approach do companies take when they need to create or redesign a product or process from the ground up to meet Six Sigma quality levels?
    a. Define, Measure, Analyze, Improve, and Control (DMAIC)
    b. Identify, Design, Optimize, and Verify (IDOV)
    c. Design Failure Mode Effects Analysis (DFMEA)
    d. Design for Six Sigma (DFSS)

10. The most popular Design for Six Sigma (DFSS) methodology is:
    a. Define, Measure, Analyze, Design, and Verify (DMADV).
    b. Identify, Design, Optimize, and Verify (IDOV).
    c. Failure Mode and Effects Analysis (FMEA).
    d. Process Failure Mode Effects Analysis (PFMEA).

11. During a Failure Mode and Effects Analysis (FMEA), the severity for an effect is rated an 8, the probability of a failure cause occurring during the life of the scope is rated a 10, and a process control's ability to successfully detect its failure mode after it occurs but before the customer's affected is rated a 6. What's the *risk priority number (RPN)*?
    a. 480
    b. 80
    c. 10
    d. 48

12. During a Failure Mode and Effects Analysis (FMEA), the severity for an effect is rated a 5, the probability of one of the possible causes of failure occurring during the life of the scope is rated a 7, and a process control's ability to successfully detect its failure mode after it occurs but before the customer's affected is rated a 9. What's the *criticality*?
    a. 45
    b. 9
    c. 35
    d. 315

13. Which of the following is *NOT* part of the design of a balanced scorecard?
    a. Metrics are financial and non-financial in nature.
    b. Metrics are labeled red, yellow, and green and reported on in meetings.
    c. Measurements are both leading and lagging.
    d. Metrics are only reflective of efforts around customer loyalty initiatives.

Answer Explanations

1. C: Dr. Joseph M. Juran is the Six Sigma quality leader known for the 80/20 rule, where 20 percent of the defects ultimately lead to 80 percent of the problems. This concept is also known as the Pareto Principle, named after economist Vilfredo Pareto. Dr. W. Edwards Deming is known for his 14 Points for Management that serves as a guide about what to change. Dr. Walter A. Shewhart is known for the Plan-Do-Check-Act (PDCA) cycle. Finally, Dr. Kaoru Ishikawa is known for the fishbone diagram that's used to brainstorm all possible causes of a problem so that ideas can be sorted into categories that ultimately lead to a solution.

2. D: Dr. W. Edwards Deming is known for his 14 Points for Management that serves as a guide about what to change. Dr. Kaoru Ishikawa is known for the fishbone diagram that's used to brainstorm all possible causes of a problem so that ideas can be sorted into categories that ultimately lead to a solution. Dr. Joseph M. Juran is the Six Sigma quality leader known for the 80/20 rule, where 20 percent of the defects ultimately lead to 80 percent of the problems. Finally, Dr. Walter A. Shewhart is known for the Plan-Do-Check-Act (PDCA) cycle.

3. B: The fishbone diagram is used to brainstorm all possible causes of a problem so that ideas can be sorted into categories that ultimately lead to a solution. The Plan-Do-Check-Act (PDCA) cycle is an ongoing evaluation of procedures and managerial policies leading to continuous improvement, and it is made up of four stages. The quality planning road map provides a more detailed approach to the activities associated with each of the three processes within Dr. Joseph M. Juran's Trilogy. Finally, a value stream map is a visual means to identify and analyze a specific business process within a company.

4. A: Environmental is *NOT* one of the four perspectives that metrics span across on a balanced scorecard. The four perspectives are: financial, customer, internal business processes, and employee learning and growth.

5. D: The goal of the Theory of Constraints is to increase profits by pinpointing constraints that exist in any component of the process. This theory is constructed on the premise that, in any context, at least one constraint exists that holds back profits from being as high as possible. This and other constraints should be addressed to improve profit levels. The other answers are ideas associated with lean thinking, but don't specifically focus on profit improvement the way the Theory of Constraints does.

6. C: Employee satisfaction is *NOT* one of the five principles of lean thinking. The five principles include: value, creating a value stream, flow and pull, empowerment, and perfection.

7. A: Value stream mapping is a visual means to identify and analyze a specific business process within a company. An Ishikawa/fishbone diagram is used to brainstorm all possible causes of a problem to sort ideas into categories that ultimately lead to a solution. Failure Mode and Effects Analysis (FMEA) is an approach used to identify all the possible ways a design, assembly, or manufacturing process, service, or product can fail and the consequences associated with such failures. Finally, Design for Six Sigma (DFSS) is an approach that companies take when they need to create or redesign a product or process from the ground up that meets Six Sigma quality levels.

8. C: Define, Measure, Analyze, Improve, and Control (DMAIC) is the most well-known and frequently used project methodology for a company working to improve an existing process. Design for Six Sigma (DFSS) is an approach that companies take when they need to create or redesign a product or process from the ground up that meets Six Sigma quality levels. Identify, Design, Optimize, and Verify (IDOV) is another type of DFSS methodology. Finally, Failure Mode and Effects Analysis (FMEA) is an approach used to identify all the possible ways that a design, assembly, or manufacturing process, service, or product can fail and the consequences associated with such failures.

9. D: Design for Six Sigma (DFSS) is an approach that companies take when they need to create or redesign a product or process from the ground up that meets Six Sigma quality levels. Define, Measure, Analyze, Improve, and Control (DMAIC) is the most well-known and frequently used project methodology for a company working to improve an existing process. Identify, Design, Optimize, and Verify (IDOV) is another type of DFSS methodology. Finally, Design Failure Mode Effects Analysis (DFMEA) is an application of FMEA that's useful for uncovering potential product failures that can lead to a shortened product life, product malfunctions, or safety issues during product use.

10. A: Define, Measure, Analyze, Design, and Verify (DMADV) is the most popular Design for Six Sigma methodology. Identify, Design, Optimize, and Verify (IDOV) focuses heavily on the voice of the customer and how to accurately, effectively, and efficiently translate that into a final product. Failure Mode and Effects Analysis (FMEA) focuses on the possible ways the organization can fail and the consequent repercussions. Process Failure Mode Effects Analysis (PFMEA) focuses on the possible ways a specific process can fail and the consequent repercussions.

11. A: 480 is the risk priority number (RPN). The RPN is calculated by multiplying together the severity, the occurrence, and the detection ratings (8 x 10 x 6). This number is important in determining how serious a risk is to output and, therefore, how quickly it should be addressed. Higher risk numbers should have higher priority, while lower risk numbers can be addressed after higher priorities. An RPN ranges from 1 to 1000.

12. C: 35 is the criticality. The criticality is calculated by multiplying together the severity and the occurrence ratings (5 x 7). The higher the criticality, the higher the priority the process should have in implementing an improvement or solution to eliminate as many defects as quickly as possible.

13. D: Metrics only being reflective of efforts around customer loyalty initiatives is *NOT* part of the design of a balanced scorecard.

Define Phase

Project Identification

Project Selection

Since resources are limited in every organization, it's important to select the Six Sigma project that will add the most value to the company. Each Six Sigma project should benefit at least one of the organization's strategic goals. In addition, the ways that a particular Six Sigma project will benefit a key business objective should be clear and communicated. Six Sigma projects should also provide a direct benefit to the company's customers. As the result of each Six Sigma project, a process should improve in a measurable way. Finally, each Six Sigma project should make a meaningful financial contribution to the organization. For a Six Sigma project that's run effectively, a guideline for annual savings impact is 2 percent of gross sales.

When deciding which Six Sigma methodology to use for improving an existing process, DMAIC is the most well-known and frequently used project methodology. DFSS (Design for Six Sigma) is an approach that's used when a team is creating or redesigning a product or process from the ground up to meet Six Sigma quality levels. DMADV is the most popular DFSS methodology.

Process Elements

A *process* is a series of steps that transform inputs into outputs. *Inputs* and *outputs* are part of every process. There are various categories of inputs, which include: people, methods, resources (materials), management, weather, the environment, natural causes, and measurement systems. On the other end, outputs include services and products (i.e., hardware, software, and information). For a team that's tasked with improving a process, it's imperative for them to know the starting point and end point of that process, which are known as the *process boundaries*.

Smaller *sub-processes* often make up a larger process. For example, in the manufacturing process used to create a cast iron exhaust manifold, the sub-processes involve melting scrap iron, creating a sand mold for the manifold's external shape, and molding a core for the casting's internal space. For these three sub-processes, each is also a process in itself with its own distinct steps. In addition, *cross-functional processes* may become subject to sub-process boundaries as defined by a company's geography or structure.

Benchmarking

Benchmarking is when an organization compares its business metrics and outcomes to an industry's best practice or standard. In addition, to improve its own processes, the company compares itself to "best-in-class" organizations that demonstrate excellence for a specific process. To be realistic about which practices will effectively transfer, it's important for organizations to benchmark against companies that are similar to them in size, culture, and operation. Benchmarking is essential for a company wanting to maintain a competitive advantage.

Internal benchmarking occurs when comparable industries aren't easily available or when an organization wants to share its established and proven best practices.

When an organization decides to evaluate its position within its industry, it's called *competitive benchmarking*, and it can be used when an organization needs to identify industry leadership performance targets.

Benchmarking that takes place as part of a group is known as *collaborative benchmarking*. For example, a group of universities form an association that allows its members to provide information to the association. In return, the association provides benchmarking and best practices reports to its members.

Process Inputs and Outputs

A *SIPOC (Suppliers, Inputs, Process, Outputs, and Customers) diagram* is a tool used by a Six Sigma project team to further define a project that's not been thoroughly scoped. A SIPOC diagram assists a team in finding the necessary answers when any of the following elements are unclear: finding out the true customers for a process; determining the customers' requirements; uncovering who's supplying the inputs to a process; and pinning down the specifications that are placed on the inputs.

When creating a SIPOC diagram, the team starts by defining the outputs of the process. Outputs are tangible items (e.g., a payment or a service contract) that are produced by the process. Then the customers of the process, or the individuals who receive the outputs, are defined. A customer should be assigned to each output. Next, the team defines the items that trigger the process, known as inputs. These are often tangible items, such as a request submitted by a customer. The suppliers, or the individuals who provide the inputs, are then defined. A supplier should be assigned to each input. Finally, any sub-processes, or activities that convert inputs into outputs, are defined.

Hiring Process				
Supplier	**Inputs**	**Process**	**Outputs**	**Customers**
Hiring Manager Human Resources Applicant Interviewer	Performance Test Online Application Job Posting Interview Questions	Interview Candidate Review Qualifications Provide Feedback	Scores and Ranks Interview Summary Offer Letter or Rejection Letter	Human Resources Hiring Manager Applicant Employees

Owners and Stakeholders

Process owners play a vital role in the success of Six Sigma projects. These individuals are the recipients of the project team's solutions and are responsible for managing and sustaining the improved process. A process owner can be the manager of a process or an individual who's not in a leadership role. An effective process owner should possess certain qualities, such as: being a subject matter expert for the process; having an understanding that the process isn't functioning properly and can benefit from improvements; and having a mind for process improvement thinking. They should also be someone who can positively influence team members and communicate with individuals who affect the process or who receive something from the process.

Stakeholders in a Six Sigma project are individual(s) or organization(s) whose interests can be affected in a positive or negative way by the project's implementation. There are different levels of stakeholders that are involved in a Six Sigma project. The first level of stakeholder is comprised of the individuals working on the project team itself. The next stakeholder level is the project sponsor, who serves as the spokesperson to upper management. Functional managers make up the next level of stakeholders, as they provide the resources (e.g., money and staff) to complete the project. Following as the next level of stakeholders are the C-level managers, who establish the organization's strategic goals with which the Six Sigma project must align. Next is the stakeholder level, comprised of those outside the company, which includes vendors and suppliers (for business-to-business relationships) and customers and users (for business-to-customer relationships). The final level of stakeholders is made up of regulatory agencies or groups outside the company (e.g., safety or environmental agencies) that can influence or be affected by the project.

Voice of the Customer (VOC)

Customer Identification

It's important to accurately identify all of the customers (internal and external) who are affected by a Six Sigma project. To ensure that all customers are identified, the project team defines the product or service and lists all of the associated users of that product or service.

Internal customers are individuals located inside a company (e.g., members of management, information technology employees, and operations staff) who are affected by the generation of a product or service. It's not uncommon to overlook the needs of internal customers while producing a product or service for an external customer. Internal customers should view themselves as service providers and strive to work together to solve problems, thus removing silos between departments. An increase in employee satisfaction has been proven to lead to improved customer satisfaction, which ultimately leads to higher perceptions of quality. Therefore, management should ensure that internal customers receive the proper training and equipment, as well as ongoing communication, to aid in the process of completing their jobs.

External customers are individuals outside of an organization who either have a vested interest in the company or have purchased a product or service from the company. Retailers, consumers, and shareholders are examples of external customers. It's extremely important for a company to be proactive in contacting its external customers through surveys, focus groups, test marketing activities, interviews, and the use of satisfaction/complaint cards and competitive shoppers. A company can use all of these tools to determine how external customers perceive the company and its products and services. These tools also enable the company to determine if its quality efforts are worthwhile, uncover if external customers' needs are being met, and learn about potential process improvements. Gathering this information from external customers is vital to maintaining a competitive advantage.

The Six Sigma project team also recognizes *primary customers* and names the remaining customers as either secondary or tertiary in nature. By further prioritizing customers, the project team is able to best meet their requirements.

Customer Data

There are many methods routinely used to collect data during the voice of the customer exercise. Although all of the methods are useful, each one has its own strengths and weaknesses. Therefore, it may be more realistic to use a particular method in a given situation based on the available resources and time.

A *survey* is a standardized set of questions in a structured format. They can be administered via mail, email, a web page, and various forms of social media. Surveys are inexpensive and are a way to collect data from a large number of people. However, surveys can have low response rates, provide limited information, and present anonymity concerns for some respondents.

A *focus group* is an interview with a small group of individuals (typically three to twelve) that lasts for one to two hours. They're best used when the interaction and feedback of multiple individuals is needed to understand an issue. However, focus groups are time-consuming to organize.

Interviews are one-on-one meetings with existing or potential customers. They're typically 30 to 60 minutes in length, and their goal is to better understand the feedback from clients. Interviews are good for tackling complex issues, but they're also time-consuming and require a skilled interviewer.

Observation involves visiting customers and watching them use or misuse products or services. Observations can help companies uncover information that they weren't previously aware of, which could potentially lead to the development of new products and services. However, observations are again time-consuming and require a skilled observer.

Using more than one method to collect data can also be helpful. For example, starting with a survey and following up with interviews can provide greater detail and insight into the survey responses.

It's important to eliminate any unintended bias from the data collection questions. This is done by refraining from the use of ambiguous questions or questions that allow respondents to interpret their meaning in different ways. Avoiding *complex questions* and *double-barreled questions* (those combining two questions into one) are other ways to reduce unintended bias. By refraining from the use of uncommon and vague words (or technical jargon) in the data collection questions, they will remain clear and concise to the respondents. It's also important to avoid questions asking respondents to provide their own ideas on matters. Finally, staying away from *forced choice questions* (those offering too few categories to select from, forcing respondents to pick from limited options) also eliminates unintentional bias.

Customer Requirements

Quality Function Deployment (QFD) is sometimes referred to as "the voice of the customer being translated into the voice of the engineer." QFD is the systematic approach to translating customer requirements into actual design characteristics during each stage of product or service development. For example, if a customer requirement is expressed as the desire to own a pen that produces a quality, controlled writing experience, QFD translates this into the specific design characteristics of a textured grip and low viscosity, quick-drying ink.

There are three goals associated with Quality Function Deployment. The first goal is ensuring that the spoken and unspoken customer requirements are prioritized. Translating customer requirements into technical specifications is the second goal. Finally, the third goal is building and delivering a quality service or product by aligning all efforts toward customer satisfaction. Ultimately, QFD seeks to turn subjective criteria into criteria that's measured and used to design and assemble a product or service.

The QFD process involves four phases in which matrices are used to capture and translate customer requirements from the initial planning stage through the final production control. The first phase is *product planning* and is led by the marketing group. The matrix that's created during this phase is known as the *House of Quality* because of its appearance. It captures customer specifications, customer evaluations of competitive products/services, product/service measurements, measures of competing products/services, and the company's technical ability to meet each customer specification. Obtaining accurate data during the first phase is critical to the remainder of the QFD process.

It's also important to note that the House of Quality matrix captures the relative importance (to the customer) of all specifications in the form of *weightings*. These weightings are based on Six Sigma project team members' personal interactions with customers or survey feedback. Weightings are displayed in the matrix (next to each customer specification) in percentages that total 100%.

Product design is the second phase of the QFD process and is led by the engineering group. During this phase, product concepts are created and part specifications are documented.

The third phase of the QFD process is *process planning* and is led by manufacturing engineering. The flowcharting of manufacturing processes, and the documentation of target values take place during this phase.

Finally, *process control* is the fourth phase of the QFD process and is led by manufacturing leads and the quality assurance department. During this phase, operators participate in skills training, and performance indicators are put into effect to monitor production. In addition, the processes that pose the greatest risk are identified, and failure controls are put in place.

Project Management Basics

Project Charter

The *project charter* serves as a working document for the project team, who use it as a guide to manage the project. The project charter begins with a clear *problem statement*. This statement explains the problem that the project is attempting to solve or an opportunity that the company wishes to capitalize on. Details are included regarding the history of the problem or opportunity, the impact to the organization if no action is taken, and the gap between the current and ideal states. It's important <u>not</u> to include any information about possible causes or solutions in the problem statement. A section known as a *goal statement* is then included in the project charter describing the benefits that will occur if the project is a success. This statement is used to "sell" the project to a sponsor. The *business case* appears next in the project charter. The problem statement and the objectives from the goal statement are converted into a *statement of business value* that links to the company's business strategy. The goal is to compel upper management to spend resources on this project. The *project scope* is the next section of the charter, which outlines the boundaries for the project. A discussion of *milestones* follows, which includes defined start and end dates for key deliverables. An *assumptions and dependencies* section is next in the document, which covers events that could derail the project, as well as variables and beliefs that must be true for the project to be successful. Sections on *team members' roles and responsibilities* and a *stakeholder analysis* complete the project charter.

Project Scope

The *project scope* is a clear statement that defines the boundaries of the Six Sigma project, thus setting limits on what is and is not included in the project. The purpose of the project scope is to keep the project team focused, motivated, and aligned. Typical elements in the project scope include: the duration of the project, the start and end times, the locations, and any sub-processes that may be involved.

A *process map* is a detailed document created by the Six Sigma project team to help gain a thorough understanding of the end-to-end process that's impacted by the project. A process map can be created by interviewing the parties involved in the process or by conducting a working session with all parties present. The completed map helps the project team uncover issues and bottlenecks in the process and points out the most important part of the process that may require closer examination.

A *Pareto chart* is an important Six Sigma project tool consisting of a vertical bar graph with independent variables shown on the x-axis and dependent variables shown as the heights of the bars. The values on the graph are shown from left to right in decreasing order of relative frequency. This type of chart is very helpful in pointing out the problems that need to be addressed first by the project team.

Project Metrics

There are different types of *metrics* associated with Six Sigma projects. *Primary metrics* (also known as *process metrics*) are established to define the project goal. They are used to compare the baseline to the improvement level at the close of a project. It's important to choose one proper primary metric within the project scope to ensure the project remains in control.

Metrics that quantify positive side effects resulting from a process improvement after accomplishing a primary metric are known as *secondary metrics*. In most cases, secondary metrics track progress in areas that aren't affected directly by the project. For example, the primary metric for a Six Sigma project may be to reduce the lead time for an offer, while the related secondary metric may be to reduce the number of offers in progress at any one time.

Finally, *consequential metrics* are used to measure negative side effects that may unintentionally result from Six Sigma projects, such as process defects or problems. It's important to note that there can be multiple consequential metrics resulting from improving one primary metric.

Project Planning Tools

A *Gantt chart* is a horizontal bar chart that's used to plan and schedule the steps of a Six Sigma project. Each horizontal bar on the chart represents an activity, and the bar's length shows the start and end points as well as the time it takes to complete the activity.

The *critical path method (CPM)* helps to control the project's work by indicating the *critical path* of the process. This is done by designating tasks as "critical" and "non-critical" to prevent bottlenecks and time frame problems. First, the required tasks are listed in an ordered sequence. A flowchart is then created to show each task in relation to the other tasks. The critical and non-critical paths are identified, and completion times for each of the tasks are determined. Finally, alternatives are researched for the critical paths to ensure that the project can be completed within the allotted time.

Program evaluation and review technique (PERT) charts are used to schedule, organize, and coordinate project tasks. This type of chart uses a network diagram of *numbered nodes* (typically circular in nature) representing project milestones that are linked together by *labeled vectors* (directional lines) representing project tasks. Since the PERT chart clearly demonstrates task dependencies, it's sometimes preferred over the Gantt chart.

Project Documentation

There are several types of data needed to properly document a Six Sigma project. They typically include:
- A project charter that contains:
  - Problem statement
  - Goals and objectives
  - Business case
  - Project scope
  - Key project milestones
  - List of deliverables
  - Project team members' roles and responsibilities
  - Project sponsors and stakeholders
- A project budget
- The project's metrics
- A risk analysis
- A project management plan made up of:
  - Project plans and schedules
- Weekly status updates
- A project closeout report

Various presentation tools can be used by the project team to prepare for phase reviews and management updates. For example, *storyboard presentations* provide a visual summary of the project's progress. The storyboard is divided into five chapters to reflect the phases of DMAIC and demonstrates the phase the project team is currently in. Storyboards are helpful when it's easier to provide an update with charts and figures instead of explaining it in words. In addition, Excel® spreadsheets can serve as another tool for summarizing project results.

Project Risk Analysis

Risk analysis is an important tool that assists the project team in identifying threats and better managing risk. It also helps minimize any negative consequences that might occur and impact the project. The first step in a risk analysis is to identify any existing possible threats. Examples of these can include: the illness or exit of a key project team member; a natural disaster; a change in a government policy that directly affects the company; an operational disruption (such as a failure in the distribution channel); or the project going over budget. The potential impact of the risk on project goals, schedules, resources, and costs must be considered as well as the effect on various stakeholders.

Once the threats are properly identified, the next step involves calculating the likelihood of the threats occurring and the possible associated impact. This is done by calculating the *risk value*. The risk value is obtained by estimating the probability of each threat occurring, and then multiplying that percentage by the dollar amount it costs the company to neutralize that risk. For example, a company identifies a threat related to the rent for one of its properties increasing by $10,000 a month in the coming year. It's determined that there's a 60 percent chance of the threat occurring. The risk value is .60 (probability of the event) x $120,000 (the cost of event over the next year or [$10,000 x 12 months]) = $72,000 (the risk value). By calculating the individual risk values, the team can decide which threats to focus on.

The next step in the process is to look at ways to effectively manage risk, keeping both cost and feasibility in mind. This can be done in a variety of ways, including: avoiding the risk by passing over a project or bypassing a high-risk activity; sharing the risk with a third party, or with other teams or organizations; or accepting the risk (when it can't be prevented or the potential gain is worth it) while attempting to reduce the impact by implementing preventative and detective actions.

Project Closure

Project closure is an important step in the project management process. First, a project closure report is created listing the activities that must be undertaken to close out the project. Next, the project resources are released, and the project closure is communicated to all stakeholders. Many project teams also hold "milestone parties" following the completion of a large project to celebrate the team's successes.

The final step is to conduct an evaluation one to three months following the project closure, which is known as a *post implementation review (PIR)*. The purpose of the evaluation is to determine the success of the project, along with documenting any lessons learned to reference for future projects. An independent individual typically oversees the evaluation to ensure it remains unbiased. During the evaluation, the project performance is reviewed to determine if the project stayed within scope, met the objectives, stayed within or under budget, and produced deliverables on the scheduled dates. Finally, a high-level report-out is typically shared with key members of the organization, which includes a summary of the project and any additional opportunities for improvement.

Management and Planning Tools

There are numerous management and planning tools that can be used throughout a Six Sigma project. *Affinity diagrams* are helpful when organizing information after a brainstorming session since they're used to organize large numbers of facts or ideas into categories using group consensus. When creating an affinity diagram, individual ideas are recorded on sticky notes placed on a large table. The team works to rearrange the sticky notes (that contain related ideas) until all of the notes are in smaller groups. Headings that capture the overall meaning of the ideas contained in these smaller groups are then determined by the participants.

Interrelationship digraphs demonstrate "cause-and-effect relationships" to assist a project team with analyzing the links in a complex situation. An example of this is a project team trying to decide which area to tackle that will have the greatest impact on process improvement. When creating an interrelationship digraph, the project team crafts a statement explaining the issue the digraph will explore and puts that at the top of a large sheet of paper. The team then brainstorms ideas about that issue and writes them down on index cards. One at a time, each idea is presented on the sheet of paper to determine if it's related to any of the previous ideas. Related ideas are placed near each other. In addition, it's important to ask if each idea influences or causes any other idea. If it does, an arrow is drawn to the idea that it influences or causes. The team then analyzes the digraph to determine the key ideas. The key ideas have the greatest number of arrows coming in and out of them. The *basic causes* are the ideas that have mainly outgoing arrows, and the *final effects* are the ideas that have mainly ingoing arrows.

Tree diagrams get their name from their physical appearance, since the resulting diagram has many branches (*subconcepts*) shooting out from a central trunk (*main concept*). These diagrams are used to successively break down and analyze a process into increasingly finer levels of detail, and they can be a good tool for a project team to use when trying to determine the root cause of a problem.

Prioritization matrices can help project teams organize data, as well as prioritize processes and resources, by showing relationships between ideas or issues. A prioritization matrix is typically *L-shaped* and is made up of comparisons between established criteria and options. An example would be rating various suppliers on established criteria, such as costs, commitment to delivery dates, and technology growth. To be effective, time must be spent on clearly defining the criteria and options, and a weighting scheme must also be applied. This tool is not used frequently since it's a meticulous method that requires skill to be effective.

Matrix diagrams can be useful when needing to show relationships between two or more groups of information. Depending on the number of groups to be compared, there are different possible matrix shapes. An *L-shaped matrix* is used to compare two groups of items to each other. A *T-shaped matrix* is used to compare three groups of items to each other, where groups two and three are related to group one. However, groups two and three <u>are not</u> related to each other. A *Y-shaped matrix* is used to compare three groups of items to each other, where each of the three groups is related to the other two groups in a circular fashion. A *C-shaped matrix* is used to compare three groups of items to each other simultaneously in 3-D. Finally, an *X-shaped matrix* is used to compare four groups of items to each other, where each group is related to two other groups in a circular fashion.

A *Process Decision Program Chart (PDPC)* is used to identify elements that can go wrong in a proposed plan that is large, must be completed on schedule, and has a high price of failure. The project team starts by creating a tree diagram of the proposed plan and brainstorming everything that can go wrong with each task. Then the potential problems are reviewed, and any improbable and inconsequential ones are discarded. Possible countermeasures are discussed for the remaining problems, including time, cost, implementation ease, and effectiveness. Practical countermeasures are clearly identified.

Activity network diagrams show the relationships between the major steps in the project in sequence using nodes and arrows. It's important to note that some project steps run in a series (one step cannot take place until the previous step has completed) while some steps run in parallel (steps occur at the same time). The critical path is outlined in the diagram and determines the project's expected completion time. The critical path is the longest sequence of tasks in a project, and it must be completed on time for the project to be completed by its due date.

Business Results for Projects

Process Performance

There are several measures of *process performance* that are commonly used to drive Six Sigma project decisions. First is the process performance metric of *defects per unit (DPU)* of product. A flaw or discrepancy on an item is referred to as a "defect." DPU is calculated by taking the total number of defects found in a sample and dividing that by the sample size. For example, if 25 defects are found in 100 units of product, the DPU is calculated by taking $25 \div 100 = .25$ DPU.

A ratio of the number of defects in 1 million opportunities (where an item can contain more than one defect) is another performance metric known as *defects per million opportunities (DPMO)*. DPMO is calculated by taking the total number of defects in a sample divided by the total number of defect opportunities in the sample. The resulting number is multiplied by 1 million. For example, take a college admission form with 20 fields of information where 15 of the forms are sampled and 30 defects are found in that sample. The DPMO is calculated by taking $30 \div (20 \times 15) = 30 \div 300 = .10$. This resulting number is multiplied by 1 million, which leads to an answer of 100,000 defects per million opportunities.

Rolled throughput yield (RTY) is a performance metric that's used to assess the *true yield* of a manufacturing process. This is found by multiplying together the daily yield from each step in the process to obtain a composite yield for the entire day. For example, the first step in the process has a daily yield of 73%, the second step in the process has a daily yield of 81%, and the third step in the process has a daily yield of 92%. By multiplying the daily yields together (.73 x .81 x .92), the composite yield for the entire day is .54 or 54%, which is a more accurate representation of how the production line is performing.

Finally, costs that disappear if tasks are performed continuously without flaws are known as the *cost of poor quality (COPQ)*. In other words, COPQ occurs when processes don't meet previously agreed upon performance outcomes. Typical examples of this include: recalls and customer returns (known as *external failure costs*), equipment downtime, injuries, and scrap/rework (known as *internal failure costs*). COPQ is calculated by subtracting the minimum cost from the actual cost. Reducing the cost of poor quality helps to increase a company's profit and aligns goals and quality.

Communication

There are various communication channels that exist within an organization. In a *top-down communication channel*, communication takes place in a "downward direction." This tends to be the traditional view of communication where information is transmitted from individuals in higher positions of authority (leaders and managers) to individuals in lower positions of authority (employees). This type of communication tends to be one-directional in nature and doesn't require a response from the recipient. Examples of downward communication include an upper management presentation to staff on the company's mission and vision, or managers receiving an email from the board of directors on a new objective they're required to meet. Occasionally, differences in status, knowledge, and levels of authority can lead to misinterpretations or misunderstandings in downward communication. Since a company's success relies on effective downward communication, individuals delivering these messages should use clear and concise wording with a respectful tone to ensure that employees understand the information.

Communication takes place in an "upward direction" within a *bottom-up communication channel*. In this type of communication, information is transmitted from individuals in lower positions of authority (employees) to individuals in higher positions of authority (leaders and managers). Examples of upward communication include employee complaints and grievances, forecasts and projections, and whistle-blowing claims. In most companies, communication doesn't tend to flow as freely from the bottom as it does from the top. This is because of barriers that exist to effective upward communication. Such barriers include: managers who fail to respond when employees come to them with information or problems; managers who react defensively when approached by employees regarding substandard staff actions; and physical barriers that separate employees from their manager and inhibit communication flow. However, there are methods that can be used to improve the effectiveness of upward communication within a company. One such method is known as the *open-door policy*. This is when a manager makes it known to employees that their office door is always open, so employees can feel free to stop by and discuss any issues they may have.

Finally, communication takes place in a "horizontal direction" within a lateral communication channel. In this communication, information is transmitted between individuals who work at the same level within a company. Examples of lateral communication include two managers working together on a project, and two employees on the same team working together to solve a customer problem. Although lateral communication is great for collaborating, sharing information, and solving problems between employees working together in the same environment, barriers exist to this type of communication. For example, employee personalities and style differences can negatively impact lateral communication. In addition, territoriality and rivalry between employees can result in a reluctance to share information.

Team Dynamics and Performance

Effective teams are an important part of an organization reaching its strategic goals. Teams should be formed with consideration for the different skill sets, positions, and personalities of its members. Teams are usually made up of five to nine members with a shared goal and knowledge of the scope of the project.

Team Stages and Dynamics

There are *six stages of team development*: forming, storming, norming, performing, adjourning, and recognition. In the *forming stage*, members have a great deal of uncertainty regarding the team's leadership, structure, and purpose. Some team members are excited about the work ahead, while other team members are busy trying to determine what behaviors are acceptable to the rest of the team. The project leader may hold a team kickoff meeting during this stage as a form of orientation. When members begin to think of themselves as belonging to the team, this stage reaches completion.

The *storming stage* is characterized by intragroup conflict due to differences in team member work styles and assigned workloads, the lack of clarity in roles, and the questioning of who's in control. During this stage, a team member may be impolite when expressing frustrations about expectations toward another team member. Storming is complete when a clear hierarchy of team leadership is put in place.

In the *norming stage*, team members begin to grow closer to one another and to respect the team leader as an authority figure. A stronger commitment to the team is felt by the members, and they begin to socialize with each other. Coworkers may go out to lunch together outside of work requirements during this stage. Norming reaches completion when the group has developed a set of expectations that define acceptable member behavior.

The *performing stage* is defined by team members working without conflict to achieve the team's goal. At this point, members find it relatively easy to be part of the team. A team member may be seen taking on various roles and responsibilities as needed during this stage.

The *adjourning stage* involves wrapping up the team's activities. During this stage, the leader may hold a meeting with the team to discuss what did and didn't go well throughout the project (as "lessons learned"). Some team members are happy at this stage regarding the team's accomplishments, while other members may find this a difficult stage as they fear the loss of camaraderie gained during the project.

The *recognition stage* can be overlooked but is an important step in the development process. There are a variety of ways that the accomplishments of the team can be recognized including emails, newsletters, thank-you notes, and bonuses. Celebrating and appreciating group achievements will lead to further successes within team development.

It's important to recognize and resolve negative team dynamics as quickly as possible. *Groupthink* takes place when team members place their desire for group consensus above the desire to reach a correct decision, which prevents the team from fully exploring alternative solutions. *Free riding* takes place when a team member limits their contributions when working in a group setting and allows their colleagues to do the majority of the work. In addition, *excessive deference to authority* can occur when a group member holds back from expressing their true opinion so they can be viewed as agreeing with the leader. Finally, *blocking roles* are another hindrance to team success because they interrupt the information flow. For example, the blocking role of the "withdrawer" is a team member who's present but doesn't participate in discussions, and the blocking role of the "recognition seeker" is a team member who either dominates meetings or is boastful.

Team Roles and Responsibilities

When forming the project team, it's important to decide who needs to be on the team and what role each team member will perform. The senior executive who's supporting the Six Sigma movement within the company is known as the *sponsor*. Executives ensure that the Six Sigma project adds value within the organizational plan. The Six Sigma *project champion* essentially owns the project. They're charged with ensuring the project's success and representing the organization's interests. This individual is involved in the activities of project selection, project kickoff (in conjunction with the project leader), and providing overall support to and communication with the project team. The Six Sigma *Master Black Belt* is an individual who's a successful Black Belt with many years of experience managing several projects. This individual is charged with assisting the project champion in keeping the project on track and in training and mentoring other Black Belts. The team leader on Six Sigma projects is usually a Black Belt. The Six Sigma *Green Belt* typically serves on a Black Belt project team or as a team leader on a smaller project. Individuals who have a particular experience that they can bring to a project, but who have no formal Six Sigma training, serve as *team members*. A *process owner* is the individual who's responsible for the business process which is the focus of the Six Sigma project. The *coach* is the individual who ensures that all of the team members understand the Six Sigma methodologies and tools. Finally, the *facilitator* assists the team when disputes arise during a Six Sigma project. The individual in this role encourages team members to voice their opinions and helps the parties involved move beyond an impasse by collaborating effectively.

Team Tools

There are several group decision-making techniques. *Brainstorming* is typically performed in a group of six to twelve individuals sitting around a table. The group leader states the problem clearly, and the participants suggest alternatives within a given time period. During brainstorming, the criticism of ideas is not allowed, which encourages the participants to think "outside the box." All ideas are recorded for further analysis and discussion. Since individuals can end up talking at the same time during a brainstorming exercise, it can block the thought process for some participants.

The *nominal group technique* is an alternative to brainstorming. Again, a problem is presented to the group. However, before any discussion takes place, each individual writes down their ideas about the problem independently. Then each participant presents one idea to the group. After all of the ideas have been presented and documented, a group discussion takes place. Following the discussion, each participant silently ranks each of the ideas. The final decision is determined by the idea with the highest aggregate ranking. This technique allows group interaction, but doesn't restrict the independent thinking of the participants.

Multi-voting can be used after a brainstorming session to narrow down a large list of possibilities. The list of options is presented on a whiteboard, and each participant is given slips of paper associated with a specific number of votes (typically 5 to 10, depending on the size of the list). The participants work individually to select the five items they feel are most important, and those choices are written on separate slips of papers with the associated rankings next to them. The slips of paper are collected, and the votes are tallied. The rankings that the items receive are written on the whiteboard, and it's interesting to note which items receive both low and high ratings.

Team Communication

Communication can essentially make or break a Six Sigma project. The Six Sigma Black Belt (with input from other members of the project team) should create a formal *communication plan* that summarizes the project stakeholders, a budget for communication expenses, and a communication strategy. The *communication strategy* further details when communications should occur, the information to be communicated, to whom the information should be communicated, the format in which the communication exchanges should occur, and why the communications are important. The governance and communication roles and responsibilities for the plan should also be clarified, along with the creation of templates that will be used. It's important to keep in mind that various stakeholders have different preferences for how they want to receive project communications (e.g., text messages, emails with spreadsheet attachments, PowerPoint® presentations, etc.). In addition, information should be included in the communication plan on how risks and emergencies should be handled.

It's important for the project team to participate in daily or weekly status meetings. This allows members to share updates on their assigned tasks and discuss any challenges or issues they may be facing with the rest of the team. This also keeps everyone in the loop with how the project is progressing.

A *project status report* or *dashboard* is typically updated after the project team status meetings to share with the project sponsor and upper management. This report is a one-page summary that shows where the project currently stands with the tasks highlighted in green, yellow, and red to alert management to current priorities.

It's also important to communicate with external customer and stakeholders regarding the status of the project to continue building trust throughout the project. This can be done by a variety of methods, including press releases, newsletters, and conference calls.

Practice Questions

1. What is a series of steps that transforms inputs into outputs?
    a. Process
    b. Sub-process
    c. Project
    d. Conversion

2. What type of *benchmarking* takes place when a group of universities forms an association to allow its members to provide information to the association?
    a. Internal
    b. Competitive
    c. Collaborative
    d. Traditional

3. Which tool is used by a Six Sigma project team to further define a project that hasn't been thoroughly scoped?
    a. Quality Function Deployment (QFD)
    b. Suppliers, Inputs, Process, Outputs, and Customers (SIPOC) diagram
    c. Program evaluation and review technique (PERT) chart
    d. Gantt chart

4. Which is the best data collection technique to use when there's a desire to reach a large number of people while trying to minimize cost?
    a. Focus group
    b. Interviews
    c. Observation
    d. Survey

5. What's sometimes referred to as the voice of the customer being translated into the voice of the engineer?
    a. Voice of the customer (VOC)
    b. Project charter
    c. Quality Function Deployment (QFD)
    d. Project scope

6. What document defines the boundaries of the Six Sigma project, sets limits on what is and isn't included, and helps keep the project team focused, motivated, and aligned?
    a. Project scope
    b. Project metrics
    c. Project charter
    d. Project plan

7. Which of the following elements is NOT typically included in the project charter?
    a. Problem statement
    b. Process map
    c. Stakeholder analysis
    d. Goal statement

8. What are metrics that quantify positive side effects that result from a process improvement after accomplishing a primary metric known as?
   a. Consequential metrics
   b. Secondary metrics
   c. Financial metrics
   d. Business metrics

9. Which chart uses a network diagram of numbered nodes representing project milestones which are linked together by labeled vectors representing project tasks?
   a. Gantt chart
   b. PERT chart
   c. Histogram
   d. Pareto chart

10. A company lists a threat of the rent for one of its properties increasing by $12,000 a month in the coming year, with a 50 percent chance of the threat occurring. What's the *associated risk value*?
   a. $6,000
   b. $144,000
   c. $12,000
   d. $72,000

11. Which of the following is the final step in the project closure process?
   a. Notify all the stakeholders
   b. Conduct a post implementation review (PIR)
   c. Store all the necessary documentation
   d. Hold a milestone celebration for the project team

12. Which tool is used to successively break down and analyze a process into increasingly finer levels of detail and is good for a project team to use when working to get to the root cause of a problem?
   a. Affinity diagram
   b. Activity network diagram
   c. Tree diagram
   d. Matrix diagram

13. Which tool is used to demonstrate cause-and-effect relationships and to assist a project team with analyzing the links involved in a complex situation?
   a. Interrelationship digraph
   b. Prioritization matrix
   c. Activity network diagram
   d. Process decision program chart

14. Which tool is used to identify elements that can go wrong in a proposed plan that's large, must be completed on schedule, and has a high price of failure?
   a. Matrix diagram
   b. Affinity diagram
   c. Prioritization matrix
   d. Process decision program chart

15. Which tool is used to show the relationships of the major project steps in sequence using nodes and arrows?
    a. Process decision program chart
    b. Tree diagram
    c. Activity network diagram
    d. Interrelationship digraph

16. If 30 defects are found in 200 units of product, what's the *DPU (defects per unit)*?
    a. .30 DPU
    b. 6.67 DPU
    c. .15 DPU
    d. .005 DPU

17. A college admission form has 25 fields of information. If 10 forms are sampled, and 15 defects are found in the sample, what's the *DPMO (defects per million opportunities)*?
    a. 60,000 DPMO
    b. 600,000 DPMO
    c. 1,500,000 DPMO
    d. 15,000,000 DPMO

18. If the first step in a process has a daily yield of 80%, the second step has a daily yield of 90%, and the third step has a daily yield of 75%, what's the *rolled throughput yield (RTY)*?
    a. 82%
    b. 54%
    c. 245%
    d. 90%

19. What type of communication tends to be one-directional in nature and doesn't require a response from the recipient?
    a. Bottom-up communication
    b. Lateral communication
    c. Top-down communication
    d. Horizontal communication

20. Two employees on the same team are working together to solve a problem for a customer. They work in the same office space and talk in-depth about the different solutions they could offer the customer. What type of communication is this?
    a. Top-down communication
    b. Non-verbal communication
    c. Bottom-up communication
    d. Lateral communication

21. During which stage of team development do team members find it relatively easy to be part of the team and can be seen taking on various roles and responsibilities as needed?
    a. Performing
    b. Forming
    c. Norming
    d. Adjourning

22. During which stage of team development might a team member be impolite when expressing frustrations about expectations toward another team member?
    a. Performing
    b. Storming
    c. Norming
    d. Forming

23. Which role assists the team when disputes arise in a Six Sigma project, encourages members to voice their opinions, and helps the parties involved move beyond an impasse by collaborating effectively?
    a. Project champion
    b. Process owner
    c. Facilitator
    d. Sponsor

Answer Explanations

1. A: A process is an overarching series of steps that transforms inputs into outputs. A sub-process occurs as part of a larger process. A project typically examines one or more processes. A conversion may not necessarily include or examine outputs.

2. C: Collaborative benchmarking takes place as part of a group and is exhibited in this question's example. Internal benchmarking takes place when comparable industries aren't easily available, or when an organization wishes to share its established and proven best practices. Finally, competitive benchmarking occurs when an organization evaluates its position within its own industry.

3. B: A SIPOC diagram is a tool that's used by a Six Sigma project team to further define a project that hasn't been thoroughly scoped. QFD is the systematic approach used to translate customer requirements into actual design characteristics during each stage of product or service development. A PERT chart is used to schedule, organize, and coordinate project tasks. Finally, a Gantt chart is a horizontal bar chart that's used to plan and schedule the steps of a Six Sigma project.

4. D: A survey is the data collection technique that's best used when there's a desire to reach a large number of people while trying to minimize cost. Focus groups are interviews with small groups of individuals (typically three to twelve) and can be time-consuming to organize. Interviews are one-on-one meetings, are usually time-consuming, and require a skilled interviewer. Finally, observation involves visiting customers and watching them as they use or misuse products or services. Observations are also time-consuming and require a skilled observer.

5. C: Quality Function Deployment (QFD) is sometimes referred to as the voice of the customer being translated into the voice of the engineer. The Voice of the Customer (VOC) is what's being translated for the project. The project charter primarily exists to explain guidelines of the project (e.g., who's involved, what materials are needed, the proposed timeline, budget, intended metrics, etc.). The project scope sets parameters for what the project intends to focus on to keep team members focused on the task at hand.

6. A: Project scope is the document that defines the boundaries of the Six Sigma project and sets limits on what is and isn't included in the project, which helps to keep the project team focused, motivated, and aligned. Project metrics are used to compare the baseline to the improvement level at the close of the project. The project charter serves as a working document for the project team, who use it as a guide to manage the project. Finally, the project plan is a formal document designed to guide the execution of the project's tasks.

7. B: A process map typically isn't included in the project charter. Process maps are usually constructed later, as a tool within the project.

8. B: Secondary metrics quantify positive side effects that result from a process improvement after accomplishing a primary metric. Consequential metrics are used to measure negative side effects that can unintentionally result from Six Sigma projects, such as process defects or problems. Financial metrics evaluate the benefits of a project from a financial perspective. Finally, business metrics measure how a company achieves its major goals.

9. B: A PERT chart uses a network diagram made up of numbered nodes representing project milestones which are linked together by labeled vectors representing project tasks. A Gantt chart is a horizontal bar chart used to plan and schedule the steps of a Six Sigma project. A histogram is a bar chart that displays a group of data points into user-specified ranges. Finally, a Pareto chart is a vertical bar graph that's very helpful in pointing out the problems that the project team needs to address first.

10. D: The risk value is calculated by multiplying .50 (the probability of the event) x $144,000 (the cost of event over the next year, which is $12,000 x 12). Therefore, the risk value is $72,000.

11. B: Conducting a post implementation review (PIR) is the final step in the project closure process. The other steps listed can (and usually do) occur as part of the project closure process, but they'll occur before the post implementation review is complete.

12. C: A tree diagram is used to successively break down and analyze a process into increasingly finer levels of detail, and it can be a good tool for a project team to use when working to get to a problem's root cause. An affinity diagram is helpful when organizing information following a brainstorming session, since this type of diagram can organize a large number of facts or ideas into categories using group consensus. An activity network diagram shows the relationships of the major steps in the project in sequence using nodes and arrows. Finally, a matrix diagram can be useful when there's a need to show relationships between two or more groups of information.

13. A: An interrelationship digraph is used to demonstrate cause-and-effect relationships to help a project team analyze the links involved in a complex situation. A prioritization matrix can help a project team organize data, and prioritize processes and resources, by showing relationships between ideas or issues. An activity network diagram shows the relationships of the major steps in the project in sequence using nodes and arrows. Finally, a process decision program chart is used to identify elements that can go wrong in a proposed plan that's large, must be completed on schedule, and has a high price of failure.

14. D: A process decision program chart is used to identify elements that can go wrong in a proposed plan that's large, must be completed on schedule, and has a high price of failure. A matrix diagram can be useful when there's a need to show relationships between two or more groups of information. An affinity diagram can be helpful organizing information after a brainstorming session, since this type of diagram is used to organize a large number of facts or ideas into categories using group consensus. Finally, a prioritization matrix can help a project team organize data, and prioritize processes and resources, by showing relationships between ideas or issues.

15. C: An activity network diagram shows the relationships of the major steps in the project in sequence using nodes and arrows. A process decision program chart is used to identify elements that can go wrong in a proposed plan that's large, must be completed on schedule, and has a high price of failure. A tree diagram is used to successively break down and analyze a process into increasingly finer levels of detail, and it can be a good tool for a project team to use when working to get to a problem's root cause. Finally, an interrelationship digraph is used to demonstrate cause-and-effect relationships to help a project team analyze the links in a complex situation.

16. C: The DPU (defects per unit) is calculated by taking the total number of defects found in a sample and dividing it by the sample size. In this example, 30 defects are found in 200 units of product. Therefore, the DPU is calculated as 30 ÷ 200 = .15. DPU is an important performance metric which potentially infers how many defects may exist in the total population.

17. A: The DPMO (defects per million opportunities) is calculated by taking the total number of defects in a sample divided by the total number of defect opportunities in the sample. The resulting number is multiplied by 1 million. In this example, the college admission form has 25 fields of information, 10 of the forms are sampled, and 15 defects are found in that sample. The DPMO is calculated by dividing 15 by (10 x 25), which is $15 \div 250 = .06$. The resulting number (.06) is multiplied by 1 million, which leads to the answer of 60,000 DPMO.

18. B: The RTY (rolled throughput yield) is calculated by multiplying together the daily yields of the three individual processes (.80 x .90 x .75) = .54 or 54%.

19. C: Top-down communication tends to be one-directional in nature and doesn't require a response from the recipient. Bottom-up communication usually travels upward to employees that are in positions of upper management from employees that are in lower levels of authority. In these instances, some form of response is usually helpful. Horizontal and lateral communication refers to the same type of communication—two-way interactions between colleagues in relatively equal positions.

20. D: Lateral communication is the type of communication that's seen when two employees on the same team work together to solve a problem for a customer. Top-down communication tends to be one-directional in natures and doesn't require a response from the recipient. Non-verbal communication uses non-speaking interactions, such as facial expressions, gestures, or emails.

21. A: During the performing stage of team development, team members find it relatively easy to be part of the team and can be seen taking on various roles and responsibilities as needed. During the forming stage, members have a great deal of uncertainty about the team's leadership, structure, and purpose. During the norming stage, the team members begin to grow closer to one another and respect the team leader as an authority figure. Finally, the adjourning stage involves wrapping up the team's activities.

22. B: During the storming stage of team development, a team member may be impolite when expressing frustrations about expectations toward another team member. During the performing stage of team development, team members find it relatively easy to be part of the team and can be seen taking on various roles and responsibilities as needed. During the norming stage, the team members begin to grow closer to one another and respect the team leader as an authority figure. Finally, during the forming stage, members have a great deal of uncertainty about the team's leadership, structure, and purpose.

23. C: A facilitator is the individual who assists the team when disputes arise in a Six Sigma project, encourages members to voice their opinions, and aides the parties involved to move beyond an impasse by collaborating effectively. The project champion essentially owns the project. They are charged with ensuring the project's success and representing the organization's interests. This individual is involved in the activities of project selection, project kickoff (in conjunction with the project leader), and providing overall support to and communicating with the project team. The process owner is the individual who's responsible for the business process which is the focus of the Six Sigma project. Finally, the sponsor is the senior executive who's supporting the Six Sigma movement within the company.

Measure Phase

Process Analysis and Documentation

Processes are a set of interconnected procedures and operations that convert *inputs*, such as people, resources, methods, and money, into outputs, such as products or services. *Outputs* act as inputs for subsequent stages of the process flow until the desired result is attained. *Flowcharts* are diagrammatic representations used to depict processes, including the sequential steps of inputs, process steps/paths, and outputs.

Cause and effect diagrams are used for analyzing all potential causes or influences for a given effect or problem in various organizational situations. Also referred to as fishbone diagrams, they can provide a clear, visual representation of the factors affecting a system or process. Both positive and negative effects can be analyzed using cause and effect diagrams.

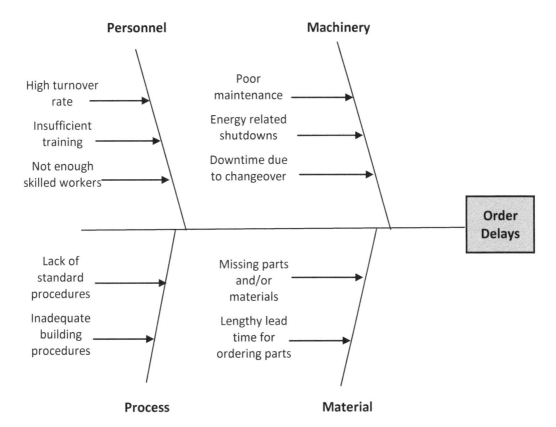

The above illustration represents a sample cause and effect diagram analyzing factors contributing to delays in custom orders. Four likely factors (material, personnel, process, and machinery) are further examined to create branches and brainstorm all potential causes. The fishbone diagram is a simple yet powerful tool that can be provided to management and other relevant teams.

Processes and their sequential steps are more easily understood in a visual representation known as a process map. A *process map* includes each step in a process, with an established start point and an established termination point. A process map also includes inputs, process steps, and outputs. The individual steps in a process map are presented in greater detail, with information about material, time, cost, and other pertinent data necessary to better understand a process. Developing a process map is often the first step taken when modifying an existing process or developing a new process; it's completed before physical implementation of the modified or new process.

The table below demonstrates common symbols used in process mapping. These symbols are used to distinguish inputs/outputs, actions, decision points, sequencing, etc. When creating a process map, the inputs and outputs often set the confines of the map; determining input and output variables is often the first step. Once the boundaries are set, the sequential steps of the process must be determined, along with any actions, decision points, documents, delays, and activities. One final and imperative step of process mapping includes reviewing for overlaps within the process. Once finalized, the map can be analyzed to streamline processes and make improvements.

Symbol	Description
▭	Indicates a process
⬭	Represents the beginning or end of a system
◇	Denotes that a decision has to be made
→	Shows the relationship between two parts of a process by showing the order in which they occur
▱	Shows output or input

A broad perspective process map analyzing suppliers, inputs, processes, outputs, and customers (also known as a *SIPOC chart*) is used for an all-inclusive view of a process or project. A SIPOC chart is relatively easy to create, and begins with establishing four or five high-level stages or steps within a process. Then the outputs of the process are determined, along with internal and external customers receiving those outputs, the inputs necessary to create the outputs, and internal and external suppliers contributing to the process. While a detailed process map includes individual steps of the process, a SIPOC chart focuses more on the details of the inputs and outputs. A SIPOC chart is especially useful when the true value or scope of the process is not yet clearly defined.

In order for a process to be effective, efficient, and cost-beneficial, each step should provide functional value. A useful tool in analyzing the value of each process step, and consequently filtering unnecessary steps, is a value stream map. A *value stream map* examines a product or service from its beginning stages (often the supplier's supplier) to its end stages (often the customer's customer). Each aspect of the process, such as inventory, labor, shipping, and costs, is evaluated to decrease waste and increase value. Typically, evaluation will include noting whether a step in the process is required (i.e. for function, by regulation, etc.), what benefits or outputs the step directly influences, and if the step could be improved. Steps that don't add value usually indicate instances of waste.

An *X-Y diagram*, also known as a scatter diagram, visually displays the relationship between two variables. The independent variable is placed on the *x-axis*, or horizontal axis, and the dependent variable is placed on the *y-axis*, or vertical axis.

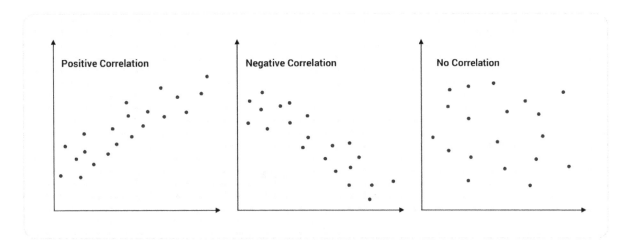

As shown in the figures above, an X-Y diagram may result in positive, negative, or no correlation between the two variables. It's important to note, however, that a positive correlation between two variables doesn't equate to a cause-and-effect relationship. For example, a positive correlation between labor hours and units produced may not equate to a cause and effect relationship between the two. Any instance of correlation only indicates how likely the presence of one variable is in the instance of another. The variables should be further analyzed to determine which, if any, other variables (i.e. quality of employee work) may contribute to the positive correlation.

A *failure modes and effects analysis* (FMEA) is used to determine factors contributing to a process or product failing and the effects of those failures. Embedded in FMEA is *risk analysis*, which includes determining the risks associated with a particular process and the necessary steps required to eliminate, or decrease, the potential of associated risks. Although this should be completed prior to the start of a project or process, this tool should be used continuously throughout the life of the process for monitoring, maintenance, and revision. The FMEA is commonly used for manufacturing processes, but shouldn't be overlooked for service and transactional processes. Some benefits of the FMEA include: identifying risks and establishing failure detection policies; assessing and improving the quality and reliability of a process; increasing process safety; and establishing a process baseline.

Probability and Statistics

Basic Probability Concepts

Probability is the chance or extent to which something is likely to happen. Generally, the probability of a particular event happening is between 0 and 1.

Given a set of possible outcomes X, a *probability distribution* on X is a function that assigns a probability to each possible outcome. If the outcomes are $(x_1, x_2, x_3, \ldots x_n)$, and the probability distribution is p, then the following rules are applied.

- $0 \leq p(x_i) \leq 1$, for any i.
- $\sum_{i=1}^{n} p(x_i) = 1$.

In other words, the probability of a given outcome must be between zero and 1, while the total probability must be 1.

If $p(x_i)$ is constant, then this is called a *uniform probability distribution*, and $p(x_i) = \frac{1}{n}$. For example, on a six-sided die, the probability of each of the six outcomes will be $\frac{1}{6}$.

If seeking the probability of an outcome occurring in some specific range A of possible outcomes, written $P(A)$, add up the probabilities for each outcome in that range. For example, consider a six-sided die, and figure the probability of getting a 3 or lower when it is rolled. The possible rolls are 1, 2, 3, 4, 5, and 6. So, to get a 3 or lower, a roll a 1, 2, or 3 must be completed. The probabilities of each of these is $\frac{1}{6}$, so add these to get:

$$p(1) + p(2) + p(3) = \frac{1}{6} + \frac{1}{6} + \frac{1}{6} = \frac{1}{2}$$

An outcome occasionally lies within some range of possibilities B, and the probability that the outcomes also lie within some set of possibilities A needs to be figured. This is called a *conditional probability*. It is written as $P(A|B)$, which is read "the probability of A given B." The general formula for computing conditional probabilities is:

$$P(A|B) = \frac{P(A \cap B)}{P(B)}$$

However, when dealing with uniform probability distributions, simplify this a bit. Write $|A|$ to indicate the number of outcomes in A. Then, for uniform probability distributions, write:

$$P(A|B) = \frac{|A \cap B|}{|B|}$$

Recall that $A \cap B$ means "A intersect B" and consists of all of the outcomes that lie in both A and B. This means that all possible outcomes do not need to be known. To see why this formula works, suppose that the set of outcomes X is $(x_1, x_2, x_3, \ldots x_n)$, so that $|X| = n$. Then, for a uniform probability distribution:

$$P(A) = \frac{|A|}{n}$$

However, this means:

$$(A|B) = \frac{P(A \cap B)}{P(B)} = \frac{\frac{|A \cap B|}{n}}{\frac{|B|}{n}} = \frac{|A \cap B|}{|B|}$$

Note that the *n*'s cancel out.

For example, suppose a die is rolled and it is known that it will land between 1 and 4. However, how many sides the die has is unknown. Figure the probability that the die is rolled higher than 2. To figure this, $P(3)$ or $P(4)$ does not need to be determined, or any of the other probabilities, since it is known that a fair die has a uniform probability distribution. Therefore, apply the formula $\frac{|A\cap B|}{|B|}$. So, in this case B is (1, 2, 3, 4) and $A \cap B$ is (3, 4). Therefore:

$$\frac{|A \cap B|}{|B|} = \frac{2}{4} = \frac{1}{2}$$

Conditional probability is an important concept because, in many situations, the likelihood of one outcome can differ radically depending on how something else comes out. The probability of passing a test given that one has studied all of the material is generally much higher than the probability of passing a test given that one has not studied at all. The probability of a person having heart trouble is much lower if that person exercises regularly. The probability that a college student will graduate is higher when his or her SAT scores are higher, and so on. For this reason, there are many people who are interested in conditional probabilities.

Note that in some practical situations, changing the order of the conditional probabilities can make the outcome very different. For example, the probability that a person with heart trouble has exercised regularly is quite different than the probability that a person who exercises regularly will have heart trouble. The probability of a person receiving a military-only award, given that he or she is or was a soldier, is generally not very high, but the probability that a person being or having been a soldier, given that he or she received a military-only award, is 1.

However, in some cases, the outcomes do not influence one another this way. If the probability of *A* is the same regardless of whether *B* is given; that is, if $P(A|B) = P(A)$, then *A* and *B* are considered *independent*. In this case:

$$P(A|B) = \frac{P(A \cap B)}{P(B)} = P(A)$$

Which means that:

$$P(A \cap B) = P(A)P(B)$$

In fact, if $P(A \cap B) = P(A)P(B)$, it can be determined that $P(A|B) = P(A)$ and $P(A|B) = P(B)$ by working backward.

Therefore, *B* is also independent of *A*.

An example of something being independent can be seen in rolling dice. In this case, consider a red die and a green die. It is expected that when the dice are rolled, the outcome of the green die should not depend in any way on the outcome of the red die. Or, to take another example, if the same die is rolled repeatedly, then the next number rolled should not depend on which numbers have been rolled previously. Similarly, if a coin is flipped, then the next flip's outcome does not depend on the outcomes of previous flips.

This can sometimes be counter-intuitive, since when rolling a die or flipping a coin, there can be a streak of surprising results. If, however, it is known that the die or coin is fair, then these results are just the result of the fact that over long periods of time, it is very likely that some unlikely streaks of outcomes will occur. Therefore, avoid making the mistake of thinking that when considering a series of independent outcomes, a particular outcome is "due to happen" simply because a surprising series of outcomes has already been seen.

There is a second type of common mistake that people tend to make when reasoning about statistical outcomes: the idea that when something of low probability happens, this is surprising. It would be surprising that something with low probability happened after just one attempt. However, with so much happening all at once, it is easy to see at least something happen in a way that seems to have a very low probability. In fact, a lottery is a good example. The odds of winning a lottery are very small, but the odds that somebody wins the lottery each week are actually fairly high. Therefore, no one should be surprised when some low probability things happen.

The *addition rule* for probabilities states that the probability of A or B happening is:

$$P(A \cup B) = P(A) + P(B) - P(A \cap B)$$

Note that the subtraction of $P(A \cap B)$ must be performed, or else it would result in double counting any outcomes that lie in both A and in B. For example, suppose that a 20-sided die is being rolled. Fred bets that the outcome will be greater than 10, while Helen bets that it will be greater than 4 but less than 15. What is the probability that at least one of them is correct?

We apply the rule:

$$P(A \cup B) = P(A) + P(B) - P(A \cap B)$$

In this rule, A is that outcome x is in the range $x > 10$, and B is that outcome x is in the range $4 < x < 15$.

$$P(A) = 10 \cdot \frac{1}{20} = \frac{1}{2}$$

$$P(B) = 10 \cdot \frac{1}{20} = \frac{1}{2}$$

$P(A \cap B)$ can be computed by noting that $A \cap B$ means the outcome x is in the range $10 < x < 15$, so:

$$P(A \cap B) = 4 \cdot \frac{1}{20} = \frac{1}{5}$$

Therefore:

$$P(A \cup B) = P(A) + P(B) - P(A \cap B) = \frac{1}{2} + \frac{1}{2} - \frac{1}{5} = \frac{4}{5}$$

Note that in this particular example, we could also have directly reasoned about the set of possible outcomes $A \cup B$, by noting that this would mean that x must be in the range $5 \leq x$. However, this is not always the case, depending on the given information.

The *multiplication rule* for probabilities states the probability of A and B both happening is:

$$P(A \cap B) = P(A)P(B|A)$$

As an example, suppose that when Jamie wears black pants, there is a ½ probability that she wears a black shirt as well, and that she wears black pants ¾ of the time. What is the probability that she is wearing both a black shirt and black pants?

To figure this, use the above formula, where A will be "Jamie is wearing black pants," while B will be "Jamie is wearing a black shirt." It is known that $P(A)$ is ¾. It is also known that $P(B|A) = \frac{1}{2}$. Multiplying the two, the probability that she is wearing both black pants and a black shirt is:

$$P(A)P(B|A) = \frac{3}{4} \cdot \frac{1}{2} = \frac{3}{8}$$

Central Limit Theorem

The *central limit theorem* states that the distribution of a sum, or average, will be normal even if the underlying distribution from which the data is pulled has a non-normal distribution. The theorem includes the following three statements:

- The mean of the sampling distribution of means is equal to the mean of the population from which the samples were drawn.

- The variance of the sampling distribution of means is equal to the variance of the population from which the samples were drawn divided by the size of the samples.

- If the original population is distributed normally, the sampling distribution of means will also be normal.

As sample size (n=2, n=5, n=30) increases, the sample mean will approach a normal distribution. Even when the original population doesn't have a normal distribution (such as uniform, exponential, and parabolic), increasing the sample size will increase the level at which the data represents a normal distribution.

Organizations use the central limit theorem because it's often impractical to collect data on an entire population, so data subsets are created and samples are drawn from the subsets. In addition, as processes aren't likely to be normally distributed, organizations use this theorem to address potential concerns within the process. This tool allows for the entire data distribution to be divided into six zones of equal distribution, known as sigmas or standard deviations.

Drawing Valid Statistical Conclusions
The field of statistics describes relationships between quantities that are related, but not necessarily in a deterministic manner. *Statistics* describes the kinds of situations where the likelihood of some outcome depends on the starting data. There are two types of statistics used, descriptive and inferential. Descriptive statistics are discussed in the collecting and summarizing data section. Because it's often unrealistic or cost-prohibitive to perform a study based on an exhaustive population, organizations can conduct studies based on a sample and use the data to make inferences about the entire population from which the sample was drawn. This is known as *inferential statistics*, also referred to as analytical statistics.

Inferential statistics help to analyze the strength of the relationship between the independent and dependent variables being tested. This, in turn, will help assess the effects of various process inputs on outputs, organizational goals, and objectives. In order to use inferential statistics, the following conditions must be met: all members of the population are known; a random sample is drawn from the population; the sample size is large enough.

The two primary inferential statistics are hypothesis testing and estimation. Hypothesis testing is discussed in detail in its own section. The most important estimation statistics are parameter estimation and confidence intervals. *Parameter estimation* uses sample data drawn from the population to make estimates of the distribution parameters to assess how well a model can detect and explain the relationship of the variables being tested within the sample data. *Confidence intervals* provide a projected range of values that are expected to contain the parameters of an unknown population. The projected range of values is determined using the sample data.

Statistical Distributions

Normal Distributions

Normal distribution refers to variable data in which most of the data points are near the mean. Approximately 68% of the data values are within one standard deviation of the mean, 95% within two standard deviations, and 99.7% within three standard deviations. This is referred to as the 3-sigma rule. The shape of a normal distribution resembles a bell, so this curve is often referred to as a bell curve. The probability density function for a normal distribution is:

$$P(x) = \frac{e^{\frac{-[(x-\mu)^2]}{2\sigma^2}}}{\sigma\sqrt{2\pi}}$$

μ= mean

σ= standard deviation

The standard normal distribution has a mean of 0, a standard deviation of 1, and the total area under its curve is 1.

Normal Distribution with Labelled Z-Scores

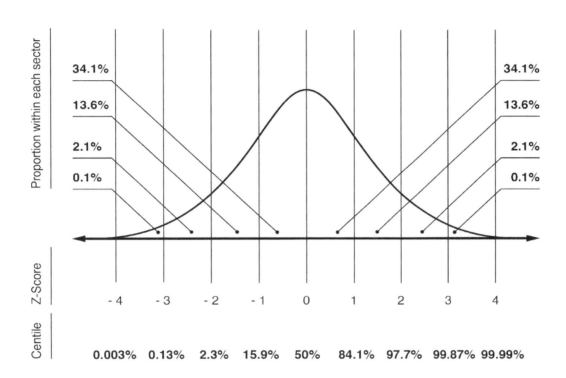

Z-scores for a point in a normal distribution measure the number of standard deviations the value is from the mean. They are used to find the area between two points on a curve. A z-score can be calculated using the formula: $z = \frac{(x-\mu)}{\sigma}$. Comparing the total area under the curve to the area between two points on the curve can determine the probability that a random data point lies between these two points.

Normal probability plots identify if a sample data set approximates a normal distribution. Normal distribution is a base assumption for certain statistical analyses and inferences. Therefore, testing for normality is important. The axes of the normal probability plot consist of the sample data and normal order statistic medians. If the data models normality, the points will form a linear pattern. The closer the points are to forming a straight line, the closer the data set is to a normal distribution.

Binomial distribution

Binomial distributions are used with discrete data. These are scenarios with only two possible outcomes (yes or no, acceptable, or defective, etc.). A binomial distribution describes the probability of a specific number of outcomes (*x*), given a sample size (*n*) and the rate of the outcome in the population (*p*). This is useful when given a specific number of trials. The formula is as follows:

$$P(x) = \frac{n!}{x!\,(n-x)!} p^x (1-p)^{n-x}$$

The binomial distribution has conditions. First, it should only be used if the population (*N*) is greater than 50. Also, it's best used when the sample size (*n*) is less than 10% of the population (*N*).

Poisson distributions

Poisson distributions are similar to binomial distributions but describe the probability of the number of events (independent of previous events) within a certain time frame, given the average rate. This is calculated using this formula:

$$P(x) = \frac{e^{-\lambda}\lambda^x}{x!}$$

λ= the mean of the distribution

Chi-Square Distributions

Chi-square distributions measure the difference between actual and estimated amounts and are most commonly used in inferential statistics. More specifically, chi-square distributions, also referred to as x^2 distributions, are the sum of squared z-scores, or normal deviates. The number of z-scores, or normal deviates, being summed equals the degrees of freedom. The chi-square distribution begins to reflect a normal distribution as the degrees of freedom increase. This distribution, however, is not symmetrical like a normal distribution.

The chi-square test analyzes: the fit of the distribution for the selected population; the independence or association of two variables; and whether the distributions of two or more populations are equal.

T Distributions

A *T distribution* is a continuous probability distribution represented by the following equation:

$$t = \frac{x}{\sqrt{\frac{y}{k}}}$$

The random variable with a normal distribution is represented by x, and the random variable with an x^2 distribution is represented by y, with k degrees of freedom.

The following assumptions are used with T distributions: the population is normally distributed; the sample size is small; the standard deviation is unknown; the mean is zero, similar to normal distributions; the distribution is flatter than a normal distribution; the distribution represents a normal distribution as the sample size increases.

F Distributions

Like T distributions, *F distributions* are continuous probability distributions that measure variances in hypothesis testing and analysis of variances (ANOVA), which are discussed in the hypothesis testing section. An F distribution is the ratio of two variances with normally distributed populations with the following equation and variables:

$$F = \frac{\dfrac{x_1}{v_1}}{\dfrac{x_2}{v_2}}$$

Here, x_1 and x_2 are independent chi-square variables with v_1 and v_2 degrees of freedom respectively.

Collecting and Summarizing Data

Types of Data and Measurement Scales

Quantitative data (information that can be measured) include continuous data and discrete data. *Continuous data* have an infinite number of values that form a continuum, such as temperature, height, weight, length, and time. *Discrete data* have finite values that can be measured, such as the number of students taking a math class, the number of responses to a survey, and the number of golf balls in a bucket. One should include continuous data measurements whenever feasible because slight changes in date and processes may not be measurable in discrete data but may be observed in continuous data. Furthermore, discrete data require larger sample sizes in order to achieve equivalent risk levels.

There are four scales of measurement which are used to define and categorize values and numbers found in data.

- Nominal: Values of the scale are used as identifiers rather than the "numeric" way
- Ordinal: Represents rank order or some other ordered series with indeterminate intervals between scale values
- Interval: Represents quantity and has equal intervals within the scale
- Ratio: Similar to the interval scale, but with an absolute zero (with no numbers below zero)

Sampling and Data Collection Methods

Sampling involves selecting values, or a sample, from a larger population and using that sample to measure, analyze, and make improvements in organizational processes. *Random sampling* simply entails selecting a value at random from the population, so that every unit in the population has an equal chance of being included. Random sampling is a fairly simple and cost-effective method often used when little information can be obtained about the population. *Sequential sampling* is often used in quality-control testing where a higher cost is associated with testing units in the sample. With a sequential sample, however, the sample size isn't fixed and involves testing the units one by one. Data are collected and analyzed as testing is completed, and the sample is concluded once the desired observations have been made. Testing in a sequential approach can lead to the desired observations sooner than with some other methods. *Stratified sampling* is used when there is no conformity within a population, and the population must first be subdivided into smaller populations before samples can be taken. Once the population is subdivided, then a random sample approach is taken. For example, if a population consists of a mixture of parts or raw materials, it must first be divided and organized in order for testing to be completed on similar units.

Data collection methods refer to the different ways in which data can be obtained and compiled. Some examples are surveys, focus groups, interviews, and automatic or manual data capture. When manual data entry is required, *data coding* is used to avoid errors. Data coding transforms data into a more easily categorized format and can also be used to protect confidentiality. Decoding involves translating the code back into the actual data. *Check sheets* are utilized to document and collect data in real time during observation of the process or procedure. The usage of sheets with categories already present and an easy to follow format allows for more efficient data collection.

Descriptive Statistics

Descriptive statistics offer an understanding of properties of a data set. Descriptive statistics involves analyzing a collection of data to describe its broad properties such average (or mean), what percent of the data falls within a given range, and other such properties. An example of this would be taking all of the test scores from a given class and calculating the average test score. Descriptive statistics entails examining the center, spread, and shape of the sample data.

Center
The *center* of the sample set can be represented by its mean, median, or mode. The *mean* is the average of the data set and is calculated by adding the data values and dividing by the sample size. The *median* is the value of the data point in the middle of the set when the sample is arranged in numerical order. If the sample has an even number of data points, the mean of the two middle values is the median. The *mode* is the value that appears most often in a data set. Note, it's possible to have multiple modes (if different values repeat equally as often) or no mode (if no value is repeated).

Spread
Methods for determining the spread of the sample include calculating the range and standard deviation for the data. The *range* is calculated by subtracting the lowest value from the highest value in the set. The *standard deviation* of the sample can be calculated using the formula:

$$= \sqrt{\frac{\Sigma(x - \bar{x})^2}{n - 1}}$$

$\bar{x}$ = sample mean
n = sample size

Shape
The shape of the sample when displayed as a histogram or frequency distribution plot helps determine if the sample is normally distributed, symmetrical, or skewed (asymmetrical); the shape can also indicate the sample's level of kurtosis. *Kurtosis* is a measure of whether the data are heavy-tailed (high number of outliers) or light-tailed (low number of outliers).

Graphical Methods

Six Sigma projects may use a variety of charts, plots, and diagrams to analyze data sets. Each method has specific applications for interpreting properties of the given set. These methods include frequency distributions such as histograms or stem-and-leaf plots, box-and-whisker plots, run charts, scatter diagrams, and normal probability plots.

Frequency Distributions

A *frequency distribution* communicates the number of outcomes within a partial range of the data set. When displayed as a bar graph or histogram, it can visually indicate the spread and distribution of the data. A histogram resembling a bell curve approximates a normal distribution. A frequency distribution can also be displayed as a *stem-and-leaf plot*, which arranges data in numerical order and displays values similar to a tally chart with the stem being a range within the set and the leaf indicating the exact value. (Ex. stems are whole numbers and leaves are tenths.)

The plot provides more detail about individual data points and allows for easy identification of the median, as well as any repeated values in the set.

Box-and-Whisker Plots

A *box-and-whisker plot* displays the quartiles, as well as the minimum and maximum of a data set. The "box" consists of values for the first and third quartiles (Q_1 and Q_3) as its "top" and "bottom". The second quartile (Q_2) is a dividing line inside the box. Q_2 is the median of the set and Q_1 and Q_3 are the medians of the values below Q_2 and the values above Q_2, respectively. The "whiskers" extend to the farthest value within the upper and lower extremes of the set.

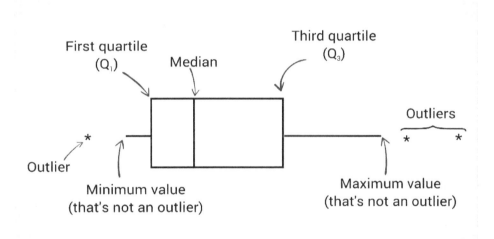

The upper extreme is calculated by adding one and a half times the interquartile range (Q_3-Q_1) to Q_3 (upper extreme=Q_3+1.5(Q_3- Q_1)). Similarly, the lower extreme extends to Q_1-1.5(Q_3- Q_1). Outliers are values that don't fall within the upper or lower extreme and are plotted accordingly. The box-and-whisker plot divides the data set into four equal quartiles and allows for quick identification of distribution, symmetry, and outliers.

Run Charts

A *run chart* is a visual display of process data that can determine causes of variation. The data points are plotted in time sequence with a reference line drawn horizontally through the median. Identifying clusters and other trends can lead to attributing defects, reduced efficiency, and other variances to time of day, operator error, machine wear, etc.

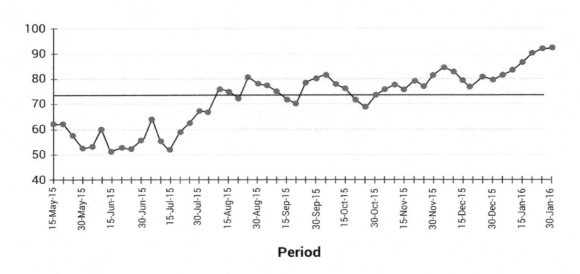

Scatter Diagram

Scatter diagrams are intended to determine whether correlation exists between two variables. The horizontal (*x*) axis represents the independent variable, and the vertical (*y*) axis represents the dependent variable. If the points model a linear relationship (a line of best-fit can be drawn through the points with the points relatively close on either side), then a correlation is said to exist. If the line of best-fit has a positive slope (*y*-values increase as *x*-values increase), then the variables have a positive correlation. If the line of best-fit has a negative slope (*y*-values decrease as *x*-values increase), then a negative correlation exists. If a line of best-fit cannot be drawn, then no correlation exists. A positive or negative correlation can also be categorized as strong or weak, depending on how closely the points are grouped around the line of best fit. This is measured by the correlation coefficient, *r*, which always satisfies $-1 \leq r \leq 1$ (*r* is between -1 and 1), where *r* is positive for a positive correlation and negative for a negative correlation. The value of *r* can be found using this formula:

$$r = \frac{\sum xy - \frac{\sum x \sum y}{N}}{\sqrt{\left(\sum x^2 - \frac{(\sum x)^2}{N}\right)\left(\sum y^2 - \frac{(\sum y)^2}{N}\right)}}$$

N= the number of data points. Remember that a correlation between variables doesn't indicate a cause-and-effect relationship.

Measurement System Analysis

Measurement System Analysis (MSA) has become increasingly used in the industrial world to reduce variation. All data in the process are essentially subjected to the measurement system so any error in the system would affect the data and could skew conclusions about the process. In general, a system is considered acceptable if the error rate is under 10% and unacceptable if the error rate is above 30%. Between 10% and 30%, the system may be acceptable depending on the application of the measurements, costs, etc.

MSA is aimed at quantifying the accuracy of the system when measurements are compared to their accepted reference values, or true values. It also determines the precision of repeated measurements when compared to each other. If a system is accurate and precise, the measurements are close to the true values and close to each other. It's possible for a measurement system to be accurate but not precise or precise but not accurate. It's also possible for the system to be neither precise nor accurate. If a system is either not accurate, not precise, or neither, the data it measures aren't reliable. There are three components to the accuracy of a measurement system: bias, linearity, and stability. The precision of the system has two components: repeatability and reproducibility.

Bias, Linearity, and Stability

Bias is a measure of the differences between the average measurement values and the true (or reference) value of the sample. (Bias=$\bar{x}$-reference value). The bias percentage can be calculated by dividing the bias by the process variation, where the process variation equals six standard deviations. A high bias percentage could indicate poor measurement procedures, instability in the measurement device (perhaps indicating equipment wear), or an error in the reference value.

Linearity is the consistency of the bias throughout the measurement range of the device. The relationship between true values and the average of their measurement values should approximate a linear function.

Stability is the ability of a measurement system to produce the same measurement values when assessing the same sample over time. An average of 10 measurements of the same sample in a controlled environment can be used to create a master sample. This same measurement should then be taken three to five times over at least 20 periods and compared to the master sample.

Gage Repeatability and Reproducibility

Repeatability is the measure of variation in data due to measurement equipment. It can be determined by having a single person perform measurements with the same equipment over a short period of time. *Reproducibility* is the measure of variation in measurement data due to the person performing the measurements (the appraiser). It can be determined by having multiple appraisers take measurements using the same equipment.

A Gage repeatability and reproducibility (Gage R&R) study is a controlled and systematic process to assess these two variations. The study entails multiple appraisers using the same equipment to measure common quantities for multiple trials. A data collection sheet is utilized to organize the appraisers, subject being measured, and trials. The range of measurement of the same subject across trials by the same appraiser is analyzed to quantify the repeatability or equipment variation. The averages of all measurements performed by each appraiser are compared to quantify appraiser variation. The Gage

R&R report summarizes, as percentages, the equipment variation, appraiser variation, repeatability and reproducibility, part variation, and total variation. Various terms are associated with R&R studies. *Measurement correlation* is used with measurements taken at the same time from different devices of the same type. *Percent agreement* is considered when an R&R study includes attribute characteristics and results are compared with a "standard" or master result. *Precision to tolerance ratio (P/T)* is the ratio of the precision of the measurement system to the total tolerance of the process in which it is included.

Variable and Attribute MSA

Variable MSA is concerned with systems that measure a sample without a fixed number of values such as length, weight, etc. These systems are analyzed to determine their precision, accuracy, bias, linearity, stability, repeatability, and reproducibility.

Attribute MSA analyzes systems that measure a sample and assign it to a finite number of categories. The simplest scenario involves a system in which an appraiser assigns pass or fail results. Attribute systems can also have more than two ratings, such as excellent, good, satisfactory, and poor. An attribute MSA study records the measurements of multiple appraisers for multiple common parts or samples over multiple trials. The data is compared across appraisers, as well as with the reference (or true) value of the sample or part.

Process and Performance Capability

Process capability describes the effectiveness of a process in meeting its objectives. Both typical and atypical causes, however, can affect a process and lead to variations that may prevent its goals from being achieved. While typical causes attribute to process variations and therefore affect process capability, atypical causes are identified and removed before computing process capability. After removing atypical causes, natural process limits are computed.

Process Performance vs. Process Specification

The measure of variation in a process is known as the *natural process limits*, or control limits. These limits are typically set at three standard deviations in either direction from the ideal output, once a process is deemed to be statistically stable and all special cause variations have been removed. These limits are depicted on a statistical process control chart and are referred to as the "voice of the process." *Specification limits* are determined by customers and are essentially the highest and lowest limits that are considered to be acceptable to them. An example is the amount of time that a patient is willing to wait to see a medical specialist before he or she becomes dissatisfied. These limits are often referred to as the "voice of the customer."

There are several process performance metrics that are used in Six Sigma projects. These include defects per million opportunities (DPMO), defects per unit of product (DPU), rolled throughput yield (RTY), and cost of poor quality (COPQ). These were discussed previously in the business results for projects section.

Process Capability Studies

A process's ability to meet the design specifications for a product (or service) is known as process capability. A process capability study is used to determine how variability in a process compares with product specifications. This is assessed both before and after a product's release to allow for improvement in its manufacturing and design to reduce variability. This ultimately leads to product improvements and greater consistency.

It is important to first decide on the characteristics that will be measured in the process capability study. Some examples include: time, distance, length, weight, hardness, and thickness. The characteristics that are chosen should be key factors in the quality of the product and have the ability to be adjusted. Additionally, the operating conditions that affect the characteristics which are being measured should also have the ability to be defined and controlled.

The target that is set for the product's design specifications is referred to as the *nominal value*. In response to the expectations of customers, management will establish *specification limits*. The smallest conforming value is known as the lower specification limit (LSL) (or lower tolerance), and the largest value that can be acquired that still meets the expectations of customers is known as the upper specification limit (USL) (or upper tolerance). Specification limits or tolerances are essentially the range of acceptable variations that are above or below the nominal value.

When products (or parts) are found to be out of specification limits, before or after shipment, this can result in them being nonconforming or defective. There are direct costs associated with this, some of which can be significant, such as: scrapping parts, rework, warranty claims, and customer loss.

The concept of *stability* as it relates to process capability is essentially the lack of atypical causes of variation. The process is said to have achieved *statistical stability* once these atypical, or special, causes have been removed (typically a bell-shaped curve). It is recommended that the assessment of process capability should not begin until the process is deemed to be in statistical control, which means that all special causes of variation have been removed.

A process capability study utilizing a control chart is built upon the assumption that the data follows a normal distribution, meaning the process characteristics demonstrate symmetry about the mean. However, it is important to note that there are cases where processes do not follow a normal distribution. Bringing the data into a state of normality is always the goal.

Process Capability and Process Performance Indices

Organizations want to determine process capability in order to see how effectively a process meets specifications. One way of reporting process capability is through statistical capacities.

C_p and C_{pk} are measurements that are used once a process has obtained statistical control. C_p is the value and measure of process capability, which is also referred to as the capability ratio. C_{pk} is an adjustment of the process capability (C_p) for non-centralized distributions (or when the mean is not centered between the limits), which is also referred to as the centered capability ratio.

If a process is perfectly centered, C_p and C_{pk} will be equal. When interpreting the process capability, the higher the capability ratio (C_p) and the higher the centered capability ratio (C_{pk}), the more capable the process.

If it is assumed a process is centered and C_p and C_{pk} are equal, the following statements apply:

- C_p and C_{pk} less than 1.0 represent a process that is not capable, meaning it does not meet engineering specifications

- C_p and C_{pk} values equal to 1.0 represent a process that is barely capable, meaning it barely meets specifications

- C_p and C_{pk} equal to or greater than 1.33 represent a process that is capable and meeting specifications

- C_p and C_{pk} with abnormally high values (typically greater than 3.0) may signal the need to find a more cost-beneficial process

P_p and P_{pk} are measurements that are used when a process is being initialized. P_p is the value and measure of process performance. P_{pk} is an adjustment of the process performance (P_p) for non-centralized distribution (or when the mean is not centered between the limits). This is also referred to as the process performance index. The purpose of this index is to attempt to verify that a sample from the process is able to meet the requirements set by the customer. Since the process is not yet in a state of control, this information cannot be used to predict how a process will perform in the future. It simply provides information about past performance.

The following statements apply regarding the P_p and P_{pk} measurements:

- Both P_p and P_{pk} utilize standard deviation.
- It is desirable to have a P_p value that is greater than 1.5 since that will reflect a process that has less than 3.4 defects per million opportunities.
- A P_{pk} value that is greater than 1 represents a process that can meet specifications.

C_{pm} is a measurement of process capability, which is also known as the Taguchi Index. A customer's target does not always fall within the middle of the upper and lower specification limits. Instead, in some cases a customer's target is set to either the lower or upper end of the limits, and this is when C_{pm} is used. By using this measurement when it is known that a process will be experiencing a shift, no "penalty" will occur for not falling within the middle of the upper and lower specification limits. When computing C_{pm}, the standard deviation is calculated by comparing the data to the target value instead of to the mean, which is what is done with C_{pk}.

The number of standard deviations that can fit between the process average and the closest specification limit is known as the process sigma, or the *sigma level*. The more capable a process, the higher its process sigma will be.

The formula for calculating the process sigma for a specific CTQ (critical-to-quality characteristic), which is a product characteristic that meets the requirement of a customer, is as follows:

$$Sigma\ level = \frac{\min\ (\overline{x} - LSL, \ USL - \overline{x})}{\Omega}$$

min = minimum value
$\overline{x}$ = sample mean
LSL = lower specification limit
USL = upper specification limit

Ω = sample standard deviation

C_{pk} = more commonly used to measure the capability of a process than sigma level

Short-term vs. Long-term Capability and Sigma Shift

Process capability is the ingrained extent to which a process is apt to change resulting from common causes. Short-term capability and long-term capability are the two categories of process capability.

Short-term capability takes a controlled look at a specific point in time at a process's potential performance. The data that is collected for short-term capability reflects no external influences on the process, such as machine operator or temperature changes, since it is gathered over a short time period. Thus, short-term capability is indicative of a process's technology and is representative of a process's true capability. An example of data collected for short-term capability includes thirty to fifty data points, during a single shift, over the period of a week for a single machine operator. The sample obtained is free from assignable or special cause (representing only random causes) and reflects an optimal performance level. The data collected is a grouping of similar items across a narrow inference space.

On the other hand, the actual performance of a process over a period of time is what is known as *long-term capability*. In this instance, external factors – such as shift or temperatures changes – can influence the process since the data is collected for a longer period of time. Thus, long-term capability is representative of both the process controls that are implemented, as well as the technological capability of the process. An example of data collected for long-term capability includes 100 to 200 data points, across multiple shifts, over the period of a quarter for multiple machine operators. The sample obtained consists of both assignable and random causes and is more representative of the performance of a process over a period of time. Additionally, the data is collected across a broader inference space. Thus, it is easy to see why short-term variability will always be less than that of long-term variability.

Process sigma is used to compare a process's output to the performance standard that has been established. Therefore, the higher the process sigma is, then the better the process capability will be also.

Using the Greyhound bus network as an example, say there are 8,000 trips a day across the Mid-Atlantic region of the United States (number of units). Delayed departures, late arrivals, and poor ride experiences are three possible types of defects. Opportunities is the number of trips multiplied by the number of possible types of defects ((8,000*3) = 24,000). For this example, the number of defects is set at 6,000. The defects per million opportunities (DPMO) is then calculated by taking the number of defects divided by the number of units multiplied by the opportunities. Then that number is multiplied by one million:

$$\left(\frac{6,000}{8,000*24,000}\right) * 1,000,000 = 31.25 \text{ defects per million opportunities}$$

The next step involves referring to a DPMO table that contains data for both short-term and long-term sigma. The long-term data incorporates a 1.5 sigma shift in its mean over time that is reflected in the process sigma metrics. GE, Motorola, and several other companies have determined that the long-term variation falls between the values of 1.4 and 1.6, so a 1.5 sigma shift has become the typical reporting standard. Scrolling down the table, the DPMO that was calculated above is translated to a short-term sigma between two values and to a long-term sigma between two values.

Practice Questions

1. Which is a commonly used, comprehensive tool for completing a measurement system analysis?
    a. Excel graphing systems
    b. Gage R&R worksheets
    c. Minitab
    d. CUSUM control charts

2. Financial capital, personnel required, time spent, materials used, and labor expended are examples of which of the following process aspects?
    a. Project costs
    b. Project benefits
    c. Muda
    d. Just-in-time manufacturing

3. Which measure for the center of a small sample set would be most affected by outliers?
    a. Mean
    b. Median
    c. Mode
    d. None of the above

4. Estimation and hypothesis testing are the two main types of which of the following?
    a. Descriptive statistics
    b. Statistical distributions
    c. Inferential statistics
    d. None of the above

5. A box-and- whisker plot of yearly salaries for car salespersons has a Q 1 of $45,000, Q 2 of $51,000, and a Q 3 of $59,000. Which of the following salaries would be considered outliers for the set?
        I. $21,000
        II. $28,000
        III. $65,000
        IV. $85,000
    a. I only
    b. IV only
    c. I and IV
    d. I, II, III, and IV

6. According to the Central Limit Theorem, which of the following four statements is factual?
    a. An exponential distribution will result in a non-normal distribution as the sample size increases.
    b. A data set with a sample size of n=20 will result in the same level of normal distribution as a data set with a sample size of n=30.
    c. As sample size increases and approaches n=30, the distribution of a sum will represent a normal distribution, even if the original data set is a non-normal distribution.
    d. None of the above.

7. A measurement system used to quantify the mass of industrial equipment produces an average measurement of 48g for a product with a "true" mass of 51g. The same system produces an average measurement of 107g for a part with a "true" mass of 105g. What can be said about the measurement system?
   a. The system lacks stability.
   b. The system isn't precise.
   c. The system lacks linearity.
   d. The system has a poor repeatability rating.

8. Which of the following statements regarding process capability is false?
   a. Both typical and atypical causes can affect a process and lead to variations within the process that may prevent its goals from being achieved.
   b. Both typical and atypical causes are identified and removed prior to determining and computing process capability.
   c. Process capability is defined as how effective a process is at meeting the desired goals and objectives.
   d. None of the above.

9. Which of the following measures the difference between actual and estimated amounts, is most commonly used in inferential statistics, and is the sum of squared z-scores, or normal deviates?
   a. Poisson distributions
   b. Normal distributions
   c. Chi-square distributions
   d. T distributions

10. A scatter diagram is constructed to represent the mileage of a car and its cumulative maintenance cost. Without seeing the diagram, you're told that its correlation coefficient, r, has been calculated to be 0.96. What can you tell about the two variables (mileage and cumulative maintenance costs)?
   a. There is no correlation.
   b. There is a weak negative correlation.
   c. There is a weak positive correlation.
   d. There is a strong positive correlation.

11. Suppose a company would like to collect and analyze data on departmental employee satisfaction to determine if any management changes are required. The current population set for data collection includes information on 160,352 employees spanning 12 departments (marketing, sales, manufacturing, human resources, etc.), while the population isn't broken down by department. Which type of sampling method would be most appropriate for this scenario?
   a. Random
   b. Stratified
   c. Sequential
   d. None of the above

12. A sample set modeling a normal distribution for the number of hours spent training per week by football players has a mean of 21 hours and a standard deviation of 2 ½ hours. What is the probability that a player chosen at random from the sample practices at least 16 hours per week?
   a. 97.5%
   b. 95%
   c. 68%
   d. 50%

13. Which of the following analyzes and measures the following components: process steps, potential failure mode, potential failure causes and effects, failure severity, occurrence, and risk priority?
   a. SIPOC chart
   b. Process mapping
   c. FMEA matrix
   d. Cause and effect diagram

14. After analyzing a measurement system, it's determined that the measurements are close to each other but not close to the true value of the sample. Which of the following would describe the system?
   a. The system is accurate and precise.
   b. The system is accurate but not precise.
   c. The system is precise but not accurate.
   d. The system is neither accurate nor precise.

15. Which of the following statements is true about random sampling?
   a. There is a less than equal probability of all units being selected when utilizing random sampling methods.
   b. This method requires extensive information about the population being sampled.
   c. This method can be used when little information is provided about the population being sampled.
   d. None of the above

16. A problem with a measurement device would show up in an assessment for which of the following?
   a. Repeatability
   b. Reproducibility
   c. Part variation
   d. All of the above

17. Which of the following represents an example of discrete data?
   a. Employees working on an assembly line
   b. Number of defective units per batch
   c. Number of parts to a unit
   d. All of the above

18. Which of the following statements regarding process capability ratio (C_p) and centered process capability ratio (C_{pk}) is factual?
   a. C_p and C_{pk} values equal to one represent a process that is capable and meeting specifications.
   b. When a process is centered, C_p and C_{pk} are equal.
   c. C_p and C_{pk} values less than one represent a process that is barely capable and barely meeting specifications.
   d. None of the above.

19. Which of the following scenarios could be modeled using a binomial distribution?
    a. The results of credit card applications (approved or rejected) with a sample set of 60 from a total of 758 applicants.
    b. The lengths of pieces of lumber with a sample set of 102 from 508 total pieces.
    c. The number of students who passed a certification exam with a sample set of 47 from 386 students.
    d. The weight of babies born at a hospital in 2015 with a sample set of 92 from 215 total babies born.

20. Which of the following is an illustrative tool to represent a detailed view of inputs, outputs, actions, decision points, sequencing, and process steps?
    a. Cause and effect diagram
    b. Scatter diagram
    c. Value stream map
    d. Process mapping

21. What is the probability that a random data point chosen from a standard normal distribution falls between -.03 and .25? (Note that the z-score for -.03=0.3483, and the z-score for .25=.5987.)
    a. 10%
    b. 25%
    c. 50%
    d. 75%

22. Which of the following sampling methods would be utilized when a high unit cost is present, and the approach is to test individual units one by one until the desired testing results are achieved?
    a. Sequential
    b. Random
    c. Stratified
    d. None of the above

23. A six-sided die is rolled. What is the probability that the roll is 1 or 2?
    a. $\frac{1}{6}$
    b. $\frac{1}{4}$
    c. $\frac{1}{3}$
    d. $\frac{1}{2}$

24. Which of the following is true regarding P_p and P_{pk} measurements?
    a. P_p utilizes standard deviation, and P_{pk} does not.
    b. A P_p value greater than 1.5 indicates a process that has less than 3.4 defects per million opportunities.
    c. A P_{pk} value that is less than 1 reflects a process that can meet specifications
    d. P_p and P_{pk} are measurements used when a process is being finalized.

Answer Explanations

1. B: Gage R&R sheets are an excellent tool for checking the repeatability and reproducibility of a measuring system. This helps ensure that the correct data is being collected for a study, and that the data collected will be error-free. Gage R&R sheets can be found online and can often be downloaded for free. Excel graphs can display two-dimensional data, but cannot be used to show anything valuable about the functionality of a measuring system. Minitab and control charts are normally used to analyze data sets collected through an accurate measuring system, not to define the system.

2. A: Project costs aren't always limited to actual dollars spent. Costs also involve human expenditure, material expenditure, and time. Benefits are usually described as savings or reductions. Muda refers to waste. Just-in-time manufacturing refers to a methodology.

3. A: Mean. An outlier is a data value that's either far above or below the majority of values in a sample set. The mean is the average of all values in the set. In a small sample, a very high or low number could greatly change the average. The median is the middle value when arranged from lowest to highest. Outliers would have no more of an effect on the median than any other value. Mode is the value that repeats most often in a set. Assuming that the same outlier doesn't repeat, outliers would have no effect on the mode of a sample set.

4. C: Inferential statistics. Estimation and hypothesis testing are the two main types of inferential statistics, which are used to analyze the strength of the relationship between independent and dependent variables.

5. C: I and IV. Outliers in a box-and-whisker plot are data points that fall below the lower extreme or above the upper extreme. The lower extreme is calculated by subtracting 1.5 times the interquartile range from Q_1. And the upper extreme is calculated by adding 1.5 times the interquartile range to Q_3. In this case, the interquartile range (Q_3-Q_1) is 14,000. Therefore, the lower extreme is $24,000 and the upper extreme is $80,000.

6. C: As sample size increases and approaches n=30, the distribution will represent a normal distribution, even if the original data set is a non-normal distribution. The central limit theorem states that the distribution of a sum, or average, will be normal even if the underlying distribution from which the data is pulled has a non-normal distribution. When the sample size (n=2, n=5, n=30) increases, the sample mean will approach a normal distribution. Even when the original population doesn't have a normal distribution (such as uniform, exponential, and parabolic), increasing the sample size will increase the level at which the data will represent a normal distribution.

7. C: The system lacks linearity. Linearity refers to the consistency of the bias (the difference between the average measured values and the true values) throughout the range of the system. The bias for the first product was -3 and +2 for the second. As the true mass of the second product is approximately twice the first, the bias should be approximately twice as much (-6). The stability of a system refers to the ability of a measurement system to produce the same measurement values when assessing the same sample or part over time. The precision of a system refers to how close measurements of the same part are to each other. Repeatability is the measure of variation in data due to measurement equipment. In this case, more information would be needed to determine the stability, precision, or repeatability of the system.

8. B: Both typical and atypical causes are removed prior to computing process capability. Process capability describes how effective a process is at meeting goals and objectives. Both typical and atypical causes can lead to variations within the process that may prevent its goals from being achieved. While typical causes affect process capability, only atypical causes are removed prior to computing process capability.

9. C: Chi-square distributions. Chi-square distributions measure the difference between actual and estimated amounts, and are commonly used in inferential statistics. More specifically, chi-square distributions, also referred to as x^2 distributions, are the sum of squared z-scores, or normal deviates. The number of z-scores being summed equals the degrees of freedom.

10. D: There is a strong positive correlation. The correlation coefficient, r, for a scatter diagram has a value between -1 and 1, where r is positive for a positive correlation and negative for a negative correlation. The closer r is to 0, the weaker the correlation between the two variables. A value of 0.96 for r is close to 1, indicating a strong positive correlation.

11. B: Stratified. Stratified sampling is utilized when there is no conformity within a population, and the population must first be subdivided before samples can be taken. In this scenario, the current population set of 160,352 employees can be subdivided into the various departments (marketing, sales, etc.), and then a random sampling approach can be taken.

12. A: 97.5%. In a normal distribution, approximately 68% of data values are within one standard deviation of the mean, 95% within two standard deviations, and 99.7% within three standard deviations. In this case, two standard deviations from the mean extends from 16 hours to 26 hours. This indicates that 95% of data points lie between 16 and 26 hours. Therefore, 2.5% of points are below 16, and 2.5% are above 26. Adding the points from 16 hours to 26 hours with those above 26 hours (95%+2.5%), you calculate that 97.5% of data points represent at least 16 hours of training per week.

13. C: FMEA matrix. A FMEA matrix, also known as failure mode and effects analysis, is a tool that analyzes factors contributing to a failing process or product, as well as the effects of those failures. FMEA matrixes are completed by gathering all potential failure modes as well as the underlying causes and impacts of those failures. In addition, the severity and occurrence is determined, along with the associated risk.

14. C: The system is precise but not accurate. The accuracy of a system refers to how close the measurements it produces are to their accepted reference values, or true values. The precision of a system refers to how close the measurements it produces are to each other when measuring the same part or sample.

15. C: Random sampling entails randomly drawing an item so that every item drawn has an equal chance of being included in the sample. In other words, there is an equal probability with random sampling. Random sampling is a fairly simple and cost-effective method often used when little information can be obtained about the items in the population.

16. A: Repeatability. Repeatability is the measure of variation in data due to measurement equipment. It can be determined by having a single person perform measurements with the same equipment. Reproducibility is the measure of variation in measurement data due to the person performing the measurements (appraiser). It can be determined by having multiple appraisers take measurements using the same equipment. Part variation refers to the different true values of each part when compared to each other. It has nothing to do with the measurement system.

17. D: All of the above. Discrete data have finite values that can be measured and observations that can be counted. Examples of discrete data include the number of students taking a math class, the number of responses to a survey, and the number of golf balls in a bucket.

18. B: When a process is centered, C_p and C_{pk} are equal. The following statements and characteristics apply to C_p and C_{pk}: if a process is perfectly centered, C_p and C_{pk} will be equal; C_p and C_{pk} values equal to 1.0 represent a barely capable process, meaning it barely meets specifications; C_p and C_{pk} greater than or equal to 1.33 represents a process that's capable and meeting specifications; C_p and C_{pk} less than 1.0 represents a process that isn't capable; C_p and C_{pk} with abnormally high values, greater than 3.0, may represent the need to find a more cost-beneficial process.

19. A: The results of credit card applications (approved or rejected) with a sample set of 60 from a total of 758 applicants. Binomial distributions are used with discrete data with only two possible outcomes. They must also have a population greater than 50 and a sample size less than 10% of the population. Answer choice A meets all three requirements. Choices *B* and *D* involve continuous data for length and weight, so they aren't valid. Choice *C* involves discrete data but the sample size represents more than 10% of the population and is therefore invalid.

20. D: Process mapping. A process map includes each step involved in a process and comprises of inputs, process steps, and outputs. The individual steps depicted in a process map are presented in greater detail, displaying information about material, time, cost, and other information necessary to understand a process. This is often the first step taken when developing a new process or before modifying an existing process.

21. B: 25%. A standard normal distribution has a mean of 0, a standard distribution of 1, and the total area under its probability density function equals 1. The z-score for a given value represents the area under the curve to the left of that point. To determine the area under the curve between the values of -.03 and .25, subtract their z-scores (.5987-.3483=.2504). To calculate the probability that a data point chosen at random falls between -.03 and .25, divide its area by the total area under the curve (.2504/1=.2504). Expressed as a percentage, .2504= 25.04%.

22. A: Sequential. Sequential sampling is often used in quality control testing where a higher cost is associated with testing the units in the sample. With a sequential sample, however, the sample size isn't fixed and comprises of testing the units one by one in a sequential manner. Data are collected and analyzed as testing is completed, and the sample is concluded once the desired observations have been made.

23. C: A die has an equal chance for each outcome. Since it has six sides, each outcome has a probability of $\frac{1}{6}$. The chance of a 1 or a 2 is therefore $\frac{1}{6} + \frac{1}{6} = \frac{1}{3}$.

24. B: A P_p value that is greater than 1.5 means the process has less than 3.4 defects per million opportunities. Both P_p and P_{pk} use standard deviation. A P_{pk} value that is greater than 1 indicates a process that is able to meet specifications. P_p and P_{pk} are measurements used when a process is being initialized.

Analyze Phase

Exploratory Data Analysis

Variations in processes occur for various reasons; naturally, the more complex the process, the more likely variations will impact organizational success. Two types of variations can occur. *Common cause variations* are process variations that are typical, predictable due to past observations, and quantifiable. *Special cause variations* are process variations that are atypical, non-predictable, and unquantifiable. It is vital to detect and analyze process variations and understand the sources of those variations in order to streamline processes where possible, reduce waste and defective products, and employ the most cost beneficial approach in production.

There are six elements contributing to process variations that should be analyzed to understand the underlying causes. The six elements include: machine, man, materials, measurements, method, and Mother Nature.

Multi-Vari Studies

There are three types of process variations that can be analyzed: positional, cyclical, and temporal. *Positional variation*—also referred to as within-part variation—examines characteristics of individual units or products. *Cyclical variation*—also referred to as part-to-part or lot-to-lot variation—tracks variations from unit to unit. Temporal variation—also referred to as shift-to-shift variation—tracks time-related variations and changes. A *multi-variate chart* is used for detecting and analyzing processes for positional, cyclical, and temporal variations.

The figure below represents a sample multi-variate line chart comprised of a series of lines along a time scale. The five plots located on and comprising the length of each vertical line represents variations within the samples. Variations from sample to sample, however, are represented by the position of the vertical lines.

Multi-Vari Line Chart

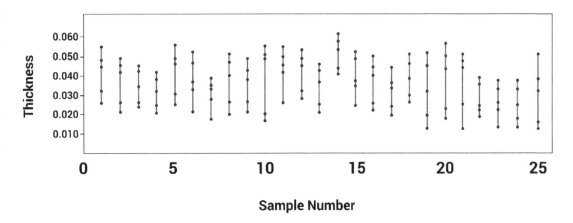

A multi-variate line chart begins with choosing the process and associated characteristics for which variations will be analyzed. A sample size must be selected, along with the values and time for each sample set. A graph similar to the figures above will include the time scale along the horizontal axis and the values along the vertical axis. Next, the observations and measurements must be plotted with respect to time and the associated values, and the values should be connected with a vertical line as shown above. The chart can then be analyzed for positional, cyclical, and temporal variations in order to make modifications and improvements to current processes. An effective follow-up strategy is conducting subsequent multi-variate studies once the process has been modified to ensure appropriate actions are taken to address the variations.

Correlation and Linear Regression

A *simple linear regression* determines how likely the value of one determined variable (x, or the predictor/independent variable) will predict the value of a second determined variable (y, or the dependent/criterion variable). A simple linear regression can only be used to examine one predictor variable. Scatter plot graphs are often used to describe the relationship between a predictor variable and a dependent variable. Predictor variable data points are plotted along the x-axis of the graph, and dependent variable data points are plotted along the y-axis.

If a functional relationship is found, the plotted points will roughly resemble the shape of a line. A line that travels from the bottom-left to the upper-right portion of a graph indicates a positive/direct relationship between the predictor and criterion variables. A line that travels from the top-left to the bottom-right portion of a graph indicates a negative/inverse relationship between the variables. Data points that fall outside of the line are referred to as *outliers*. Outliers may provide additional information about the dataset or data collection methods, as they normally don't occur due to random chance. If data points create no pattern on the graph, this indicates no relationship between the predictor and dependent variables. Some data sets may also plot as non-linear shapes, such as curves or clusters. This indicates that a relationship exists between the predictor and dependent variables, but a linear regression technique doesn't explain the details of that relationship.

A linear regression equation is modeled as $y = b_0 + b_1(x)$, where b_0 = the intercept, b_1 = the regression coefficient, x = an observed data value of the predictor variable, and y = the output to be predicted.

When determining a relationship between predictor and dependent variables, *correlation testing* can show the strength of the relationship. Correlation techniques work best with quantitative rather than with categorical data. To best determine the degree of linear relationship between two variables, use the Pearson Product Moment Correlation, commonly referred to as *Pearson's correlation*. In correlation tests, the resulting value is known as the *correlation coefficient*, also referred to as r. The correlation coefficient is discussed in the collecting and summarizing data section.

Regression equations explain relationships between data sets. They can be straightforward and simple. They can also involve multiple predictor and dependent variables that may be curvilinear, spread, or have some other non-linear relationship when the data sets are plotted. When a relationship or trend is determined between a predictor and dependent variable, it's expressed through a regression equation and can be used to create a visual model. Comparing actual data to a model demonstrates how well the data sets fit the model. For example, a good fit indicates that the sample data set is appropriate for making predictions about a larger population. A good fit between observed data points and a regression model can be determined by visually checking for the line of best fit. A more systematic approach involves the least square method, an actual equation that provides parameters to which observed data points are related.

Some important terms that may appear in analysis reports from most statistical software programs include:

- R-squared: The square of correlation coefficient r. This statistical measure predicts the percent of variation in the predictor and dependent data sets. The higher the R-squared value, the smaller the variation and deviation between the data points and the regression model. Consequently, this means the higher the accuracy when making predictions for a larger population.

- Line of Best Fit/Least Squares Method: An ideal "predictor" line to represent all points on a scatter plot that follows a linear shape. With a good data set, most, if not all, values plotted on the graph will fall close to this line. Some points may fall directly on the line. The least squares method calculates an actual line of best fit.

- Standard Error: Measures the deviation of each scatter plot data point from the line of best fit. The smaller the standard error, the better the data set.

- Multicollinearity: When two or more predictor variables have a high correlation, making it difficult to determine relationships between one or more of the predictor variables and the dependent variable(s).

- P-Value: Determines the probability at which the results of the analysis occurred by chance.

Predictions from data sets are generally expressed as contingent to a degree of accuracy. *Confidence intervals* are a range of values that express the degree of accuracy to which the mean has been calculated. They express the likelihood of a parameter of interest. A confidence interval is an indicator from and relevant to an established data set. For example, a supplier may randomly sample an equipment part to see how long that part works for a consumer with normal daily use before breaking down. The supplier may calculate a 95% confidence interval of 365 days and 400 days. This means that the average consumer can be 95% confident that the part will last between 365 and 400 days of use before there's a need to replace it. The confidence interval conveys no other information about the part except a specific quality of durability. A common misconception is that it indicates 95% of these parts will break between 365 and 400 days.

Most researchers will set a confidence interval of 95%. However, confidence intervals of 90% or 99% are also common depending on the level of known process variation or sample size of the data set. Higher variation will result in lower confidence levels. Larger sample sizes will result in higher confidence intervals. The confidence level is set in tandem with the statistical significance level of a hypothesis.

Prediction intervals use established observations to predict an approximation of what may occur in the future, or in a context beyond the sample set. This statistic could be used in the equipment part example above to predict how many parts will break between 365 and 400 days. Prediction intervals are commonly used as a component of regression analyses. Prediction intervals take the regression equation of a sample set and use it to infer parameters between which population values may lie. This is different from a confidence interval, as prediction intervals work with variables that aren't actually present in the data set. Therefore, prediction variables are almost always wider in range than confidence intervals.

Multiple linear regressions are similar to single linear regressions except that they involve more than one predictor variable. Simple linear regression techniques are extended to include all predictor variables studied in multiple linear regression functions. Consequently, multiple linear regressions involve noting errors found in the distribution of all predictor variable data sets, multiple correlation coefficients (noted with capital letter R), and the use of t-tests to examine how well the multiple linear regression predict future outcomes. As multiple linear regressions involve more than one predictor variable, matrices organize the relationships between the predictor variables and the dependent variable.

Data in a multiple linear regression must be normally distributed. Multicollinearity should be low or absent, so as not to confuse the effects of each predictor variable with one another or individually with the dependent variable. Weighted coefficients can show how strongly one predictor variable relates with the dependent variable. Multiple linear regression analyses are most commonly used to examine the influence of predictor variables on a dependent variable (examining education, geographic location, and gender as predictors of mid-career income); to examine the effects of process change (implementing a new workflow on an assembly line, while accounting for worker input, equipment input, etc. as predictor variables); and to predict future trends (predicting marketplace demand for a new product while accounting for additional factors that could also influence purchasing).

Hypothesis Testing

Basics of Hypothesis Testing

Hypothesis testing uses statistical analysis of the relationship between two samples and determines whether the differences among the samples are due to arbitrary and random happenings, or true differences within the samples and associated data. Hypothesis testing includes both a null hypothesis and an alternative hypothesis. The *null hypothesis* (represented by H_0) is a default position that states there are no differences between two samples, or no relationship between the measured discrepancies. The opposite of the null is the *alternative hypothesis* (represented by H_1) which states there is a relationship between the measured discrepancies, and that the differences between the samples aren't due to chance. A variety of tools are used to perform statistical analysis within hypothesis testing in order to accept or reject the null hypothesis. If the null hypothesis is rejected due to statistical evidence supporting otherwise, then the alternate hypothesis is accepted.

Statistical significance translates to rejecting the null hypothesis; in other words, it correlates to the probability of a relationship between the variables and samples rather than sampling error or chance. Statistical significance is represented by the p-value. *P-value* is the probability that the test statistic is equal to or less than the significance level. If the p-value is less than the significance level, then the test is considered statistically significant. For example, if the significance level is .05 and the p-value is less than .05, then the test is considered to be statistically significant. With any large sample size, differences among samples will translate to "significant" solely due to the sample size being large enough.

When differences between samples and data sets are found to be statistically significant, the next step is to determine whether the differences are practically significant. *Practical significance*, also referred to as clinical significance, focuses on whether the differences have implications in a real-world application.

In order to select a sample size *n* for hypothesis testing, the following must be determined: the desired level of Type 1 error/risk, the desired level of Type II error/risk, a required value to be detected between the means of the two populations or samples, and the standard deviation or an estimate of the standard deviation.

A *significance level* is set for each test, typically at .05. This means that there is a probability of 5% of being incorrect when rejecting the null hypothesis. It is important to note that the significance level affects power. As a test's significance level increases, its power and risk increase accordingly.

The ability of a test to reject the null hypothesis when it is false is known as *power*. Calculating the power prior to conducting a hypothesis test is important to assist in determining if the sample size being used is large enough for the test's purpose. Tests that have a power of 80% or greater are statistically highly powerful. If it is found that the power for a given test needs to be increased, that can be accomplished by increasing the sample size, decreasing the variability within the sample, increasing the alpha of the test, or increasing the difference to be detected between the alternative and null values.

A *Type I Error* occurs when the null hypothesis is incorrectly rejected. For example, if products were considered defective when they were actually non-defective, this is a Type I Error. Type I Errors are also referred to as false positives, alpha (α) errors, or alpha risk.

A *Type II Error* occurs when the null hypothesis isn't rejected when it should have been. For example, if products were considered non-defective when they were actually defective, this is a Type II Error. Type II Errors are also referred to as false negatives, beta (β) errors, or beta risk.

See the figure below for an example of a *two-tail test*, also referred to as a non-directional hypothesis, which tests the variables for relationships in either direction. With a two-tail test, the alpha error is divided into two equal parts at both tails of the distribution when testing for statistical significance. For example, if .05 is the significance level, then α = .025 in each tail of the distribution as represented by the dark blue shaded area. Therefore, the possibility of a relationship is being tested in both directions.

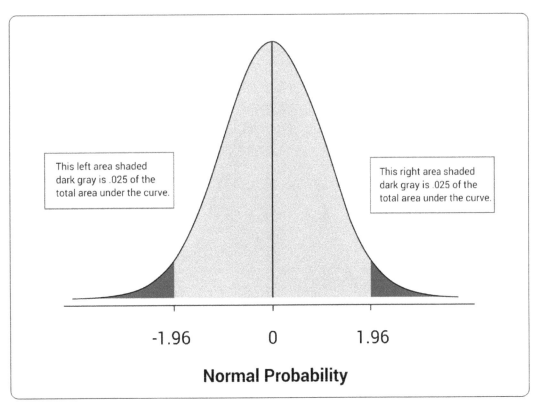

See the figures below for examples of *one-tail* tests, also referred to as a directional hypothesis, which tests the variables for relationships in only one direction. With a one-tail test, the entire alpha error is placed in one tail of the distribution when testing for statistical significance. For example, if .05 is the significance level, then α = .05 in one tail of the distribution as represented by the dark blue shaded area. Therefore, the possibility of a relationship is being tested in one direction only. A one-tail test should only be used when there is extensive knowledge about the direction of the effect, as missing an effect in the opposite direction by not using a two-tail test may prove costly.

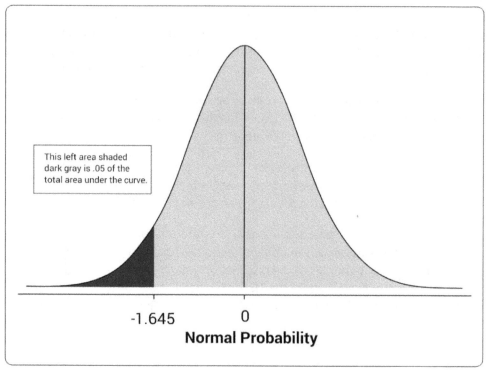

This left area shaded dark gray is .05 of the total area under the curve.

-1.645   0
Normal Probability

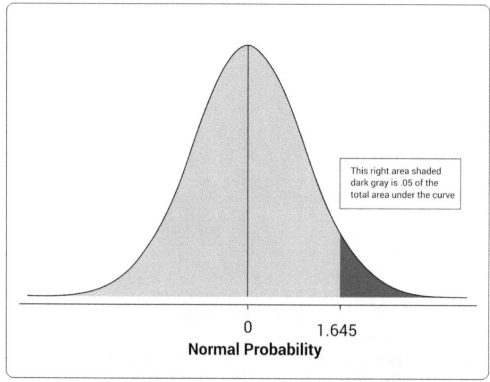

This right area shaded dark gray is .05 of the total area under the curve

0   1.645
Normal Probability

Tests for Means, Variances, and Proportions

In real data situations, a true normal distribution (ranging anywhere from negative infinity to infinity) is rare. However, if the set is close to normality, T-tests and the one-way ANOVA test can be used in testing of the mean of the set(s). Therefore, the initial step before hypothesis testing should be to test the sample(s) for normality with a probability plot on paper or statistical software with the Shapiro–Wilk and Kolmogorov-Smirnov tests.

One-Sample T-test
A *single-sample T-test* is a form of hypothesis testing to compare the mean of a sample with the mean of the population from which the sample is taken. It's used when the sample size is small (normally under 30) and the standard deviation of the population is unknown. The test statistic (*t*) is calculated:

$$= \frac{\bar{x} - \mu_o}{s / \sqrt{n}}$$

$\bar{x}$=sample mean
μ_0= population mean
s= standard deviation of the sample
n= the number of test samples

Once calculated, the test statistic is compared with the critical value (t_c). The critical values are based on the significance level (or error rate) and the degrees of freedom (*df*). If the hypothesis is that the sample mean equals the population mean, this is a two-tailed test using the significance level $\alpha/2$ (the critical value is $t_{\alpha/2}$). If the hypothesis is that the sample mean is less or greater than the population mean, this is a one-tailed test using the significance level α. The degrees of freedom are based on the sample size and calculated $df = n - 1$. A table of values of a *t*-distribution is then used to find the critical value with the given degrees of freedom. This critical value gives the reject region for the test. For a two-tailed test, the region is above $t_{\alpha/2}$ and below $-t_{\alpha/2}$. For a left-tailed test, the region is below $-t_\alpha$. For a right-tailed test, the region is above t_α. If the test statistic (*t*) falls in the reject region, then H_o (the null hypothesis) is rejected. Remember, the null hypothesis assumes that there are no significant differences between the sample mean and the population mean. Rejecting the null hypothesis indicates that the sample mean is not equal to the population mean; the sample mean is greater than the population mean; or the sample mean is less than the population mean.

Two-Sample T-test
The *two-sample T-test* is a form of hypothesis testing to determine if the means of the two populations are significantly different. A two-sample *t*-test can be a paired-test where each value in one sample is matched with a value in the other set. An example would be matching scores pre-training with scores post-training for the same individuals. For a paired test, the sample sizes for each set must be equal.

The test statistic (t) is calculated:

$$t = \frac{\bar{d}}{\frac{s_d}{\sqrt{n}}}$$

$\bar{d}$= the mean of the differences between each pair
s= the standard deviation of the differences
n= the number of paired differences

A critical value (t_c) is determined based on the significance level $\alpha/2$ (a paired test is always a two-tailed test) and degrees of freedom (n-1). The test statistic (t) and critical value ($t_{\alpha/2}$) are compared to see if the null hypothesis (the means are equal) is rejected.

A two-sample T-test can also be used for unpaired data. This can be useful when comparing two different processes that complete the same task. In these cases, equal sample sizes aren't necessary. The calculations for unpaired two-sample T-tests differ whether or not the standard deviations of the populations are assumed to be equal. For equal variance,

$$t = \frac{\overline{x_1} - \overline{x_2}}{s_p \bigg/ \sqrt{\frac{1}{n_1} + \frac{1}{n_2}}}$$

$\overline{x_1}$= the mean of sample set 1
$\overline{x_2}$= the mean of sample set 2
n_1= the number of data values in sample 1
n_2= the number of data values in sample 2

and

$$s_p = \sqrt{\frac{(n_1 - 1)s_1{}^2 + (n_2 - 1)s_2{}^2}{n_1 + n_2 - 2}}$$

For unequal variance:

$$t \frac{\overline{x_1} - \overline{x_2}}{\sqrt{\frac{s_1{}^2}{n_1} + \frac{s_2{}^2}{n_2}}}$$

Again, to determine if the null hypothesis (the means are equal) is rejected, t is compared to the critical value (t_c) based on significance level and degree of freedom. Note that the degree of freedom (df) differs for equal and unequal variance. For equal variance, $df = n_1 + n_2 - 2$ and for unequal variance:

$$df = \cfrac{1}{\left(\cfrac{\frac{s_1{}^2}{n_1}}{\frac{s_1{}^2}{n_1} + \frac{s_2{}^2}{n_2}}\right) + \left(\cfrac{\frac{s_2{}^2}{n_2}}{\frac{s_1{}^2}{n_1} + \frac{s_2{}^2}{n_2}}\right)}{n_1 - 1 \qquad n_2 - 1}$$

F-Test

An *F-test* is also referred to as the test for two variances. This hypothesis test is used when data exists from two independent samples that were taken from normally distributed populations. The goal is to determine if there is any statistical significance between the variance of the two samples of data. When there is a process issue, an F-test may help to provide insight into a root cause.

The following example uses these two samples:

	1	2	3	4	5	Variance (s)
Sample 1	5	8	10	9	12	6.7
Sample 2	21	18	24	22	17	8.5

To calculate the variance for each sample, the following formula is used:

$$s^2 = \frac{\Sigma(x_i - \bar{x})^2}{n - 1}$$

s^2 = variance
x_i = data set item
$\bar{x}$ = sample mean
Σ = sum
n = sample size

The variances are used to provide an F statistic by way of the following formula:

$$F = \frac{s1^2}{s2^2} = \frac{8.5}{6.7} = 1.27$$

An example of an F-test application is two assembly lines producing a product. The product that is produced on the first assembly line has a two pound variance in weight, and the product that is produced on the second assembly line has a four pound variance in weight. The test is performed to determine if the difference in weight variation is simply random, or if the first assembly line is truly experiencing less variance.

Z-test

A *Z-test* is a hypothesis test that is used for data that is normal distributed when the standard deviation is known. This test calculates what is known as a z-score, which details how much a data point deviates from a specification or mean.

A z-score is calculated by using the following formula:

$$Z = \frac{\text{data point} - \text{mean}}{\text{standard deviation}}$$

A higher z-score equates to a sample that is further away from a specification limit. This, in turn, relates to a higher process sigma and less defective process.

Test of One Proportion
To determine if a process is indeed performing at the level of an established standard, the hypothesis test known as the *test of one proportion* can be used. When a difference is detected between a data set and a standard, this test helps to explain if the difference is simply random or if is statistically significant in nature.

The following formula is used to calculate the test of one proportion:

$$z = \frac{X - np_o}{\sqrt{np_0(1 - p_0)}}$$

An example of a test of one proportion application is a shipping vendor that has guaranteed overnight delivery. A test could be run to see if the vendor is performing as originally intended.

Confidence Intervals
Confidence intervals for the mean, standard deviation, and proportion are based on a typical confidence level of ninety-five percent. They are calculated using statistical methods by utilizing samples to make conclusions about larger populations.

When a numerical characteristic is being measured and there is a desire to find the average for a population, this is when a sample mean can be used to estimate the population mean. This is done by calculating a *confidence interval for the mean*, which is determined by the following formula (when the standard deviation is known): $\bar{x} \pm Z\frac{\sigma}{\sqrt{n}}$ where $\bar{x}$= sample mean, Z stands for the appropriate value for your desired confidence value from the standard normal distribution, σ= population standard deviation, and n= sample size.

*Please note, for a confidence interval of ninety-five percent, the z-value is 1.96.

There may be a desire to estimate the percentage of individuals in a population that fall into a specific interest category. This is when a sample proportion can be used to estimate for a larger population and when a *confidence interval for proportion* is useful. A confidence interval for proportion is determined by the following formula:

$$\hat{p} \pm Z\sqrt{\frac{\hat{p}(1 - \hat{p})}{n}}$$

where Z stands for the appropriate value for your desired confidence value from the standard normal distribution and n= sample size.

*Please note, for a confidence interval of ninety-five percent, the z-value is 1.96.

A *confidence interval for standard deviation* is determined by the following formula:

$$\sqrt{\frac{(n-1)s^2}{x^2_{a/2,\,n-1}}} \leq \sigma \leq \sqrt{\frac{(n-1)s^2}{x^2_{(1-a/2),\,n-1}}}$$

x^2= a Chi-Square distribution with (n-1) degrees of freedom

It is important to note that the confidence interval for standard deviation will not be symmetric since the Chi-square distribution is not symmetric.

One-way ANOVA

To determine differences between the means of three or more independent groups, the one-way *analysis of variance (ANOVA)* can be used. (ANOVA can be used for only two groups, but an independent-samples T-test is more common.) An example would be comparing the average lifespan (dependent variable) of cars produced by different manufacturers (independent variable). Although the one-way ANOVA will tell if there are significant differences between at least two of the means from the group, it doesn't tell which groups differ from each other. To determine this, additional testing is required.

Before performing a one-way ANOVA, it's important to check that certain assumptions are met. If not, the validity of the results is reduced. First, if the dependent variable is a continuous measurement, it should be measured at the interval or ratio level. For example, time would be measured in years, months, days, etc. The independent variable should be independent groups with no relationship between observations with or among groups. The dependent variable should approximate a normal distribution for each independent group with no significant outliers. Finally, a one-way ANOVA requires homogeneity of variances (the standard deviations of the mean are statistically the same).

The one-way ANOVA tests the null hypothesis that all the means are equal. The variation between groups is compared to the variation within groups using the *f*-statistic. If the variation caused by the group is a sufficiently large multiple of the experimental error (α), the null hypothesis is rejected. Statistical software is useful in calculating the one-way ANOVA. If calculating manually, the *f*-statistic is compared with a critical value found in an F-table to determine if it falls in the reject region. Constructing an ANOVA table similar to the one below can be useful in calculating the *f*-statistic.

Source of Variation	Sum of Squares	Degrees of Freedom	Mean Squares	F-statistic
Between Groups	SS_B	k-1	$MS_B=SS_B/(k-1)$	$F=MS_B/MS_W$
Within Groups	SS_W	N-k	$MS_W=SS_W/(N-k)$	
Total	SS_T	N-1		

For the table, *N*= number of observations, *n*= number of observations per group, *k*= number of groups, *T*= grand total of observations $\sum y_i = \sum T_i$, *C*= correction factor T^2/N, y_i's= individual measurements, SS_T= sum of squares total= $\sum y_i^2 - C$, SS_B= sum of squares between groups= $\sum T_i^2/n - C$, and SS_W= sum of squares within groups= SS_T-SS_B. The critical value found in an F-table uses *k*-1 as the numerator degrees of freedom and *k*(*n*-1) as the denominator degrees of freedom.

Chi-Square (Contingency Tables)

The *chi-square statistic* can determine whether there is a difference between the distributions of two categorical variables across independent populations. An example would be comparing the frequency of alcohol consumption (i.e., rare, occasional, often) by college students based on gender. To test the null hypothesis (the variables are independent), arrange the data in a *contingency table*, which presents the frequency tables of both variables simultaneously, as shown below. The levels of one variable constitute the rows of the table, and the levels of the other constitute the columns. The margins consist of the sum of cell frequencies for each row and each column (marginal frequencies). The lower-right corner is the sum of marginal frequencies for the rows or the columns. (Both sums are equal to the sample size N.)

	Rare	Occasional	Often	
Male	Frequency count	Frequency count	Frequency count	Sum of Row 1
Female	Frequency count	Frequency count	Frequency count	Sum of Row 2
	Sum of Column 1	Sum of Column 2	Sum of Column 3	N

Once the frequency counts are displayed as a contingency table, calculate the expected frequency for each cell, $E_{r,c}$. (The chi-square test should only be used if the expected frequency for each cell is greater than 5.) $E_{r,c} = \frac{(n_r n_c)}{N}$, where $E_{r,c}$= expected frequency count for cell in row r, column c; n_r= marginal frequency for row r; n_c= marginal frequency for column c; N= total sample size. The chi-square (x^2) statistic can then be calculated by:

$$x^2 = \sum \frac{(O_{r,c} - E_{r,c})^2}{E_{r,c}}$$

$O_{r,c}$= the observed frequency count for the cell in row r, column c. The calculated value for x^2 is compared to a critical value obtained from a chi-square distribution table. The critical value is based on the significance level and degrees of freedom (df), calculated $df = (r-1)(c-1)$ where r= the number of rows and c= the number of columns. If the test statistic is greater than the critical value, the null hypothesis is rejected, as the variables tested aren't independent.

This section discusses how to use data collected to solve a manufacturing or organizational problem determined by a root cause or gap analysis. It's important to understand the relationships and trends that exist within data sets. The descriptive statistic techniques explained in this section can be calculated and illustrated in spreadsheet software, such as Microsoft Excel, or statistical software programs, such as IBM SPSS Statistics, Minitab, Stata, and MaxStat.

Practice Questions

1. Minitab and Stata are all examples of which of the following?
   a. Statistical software
   b. Spreadsheet software
   c. Statistical theorems
   d. Software automation

2. Which of the following describes a tool utilized for testing the variables for relationships in either direction, and divides the alpha error into two equal parts within the distribution when testing for statistical significance?
   a. Binomial distribution
   b. Poisson distribution
   c. Two-tail test
   d. None of the above

3. A line that travels from the bottom-left of a graph to the upper-right of the graph indicates what kind of relationship between a predictor and a dependent variable?
   a. Positive
   b. Negative
   c. Exponential
   d. Logarithmic

4. What does a correlation coefficient of 1 indicate between a predictor variable and a dependent variable?
   a. No relationship
   b. The strongest possible positive relationship
   c. The predictor variable directly causes the presence of the outcome being studied
   d. A non-linear relationship, usually in a parabolic shape

5. Which of the following indicate the notation used for the correlation coefficient in a simple regression analysis and a multiple regression analysis, respectively?
   a. Sigma, Six Sigma
   b. Theta, Pi
   c. r, R
   d. s, S

6. Which of the following terms describes when two or more predictor variables have a high correlation, making it difficult to determine relationships between one or more predictor variables and the dependent variable(s)?
   a. Multiple regression
   b. Statistical noise
   c. Significant confusion
   d. Multicollinearity

7. When a data set plots as a non-linear shape (such as a cluster or curve), what does this indicate about the relationship between the predictor and dependent variables?
    a. There's a negative/inverse relationship between the variables.
    b. Some points in the data set are identified as outliers.
    c. There's a positive/direct relationship between the variables.
    d. A relationship exists between the variables, but a linear regression technique cannot explain it.

8. Which of the following is an example of cyclical process variation?
    a. Product-to- product variation
    b. Part-to- part variation
    c. Within-part variation
    d. Shift-to- shift variation

9. Which of the following hypothesis tests requires equal sample sizes?
    a. Two-sample proportion test
    b. One-way ANOVA test
    c. Paired T-test
    d. All of the above

10. Which of the following accurately describes a multi-variate line chart used for detecting and tracking process variations?
    a. The time scale is placed along the vertical axis, and the values are placed along the horizontal axis; the length of each vertical line represents variations within the samples.
    b. The time scale is placed along the horizontal axis, and the values are placed along the vertical axis; the position of vertical lines represents variations within the samples.
    c. The time scale is placed along the vertical axis, and the values are placed along the horizontal axis; the position of vertical lines represents variations from sample to sample.
    d. None of the above.

11. A toothpaste company proclaims that 90% of U.S. dentists recommend their brand. You poll a random sample of 100 dentists with 83 recommending this particular brand. Which test can be used to determine if the company's statement is false?
    a. One-sample proportion test
    b. Two-sample proportion test
    c. Paired t-test
    d. One sample t-test

12. Which of the following indicates a false positive, occurring when the null hypothesis is incorrectly rejected?
    a. Type II error
    b. Beta error
    c. Type I error
    d. Beta risk

13. If products were considered non-defective when in actuality the products were defective, it's an example of which of the following?
    a. Type II error
    b. Alpha risk
    c. Type I error
    d. False positive

14. If the significance level is .05 and the p-value is .02, then the test is considered to be which of the following?
    a. Not statistically significant
    b. Statistically significant
    c. A or B may apply; more information is required
    d. None of the above

15. Which of the following scenarios can be tested using the chi-square test for a contingency table?
    a. Comparing the marital status of adults of different ethnic groups.
    b. Comparing the average length of marriage of different ethnic groups.
    c. Comparing the number of injuries per month at different manufacturing plants.
    d. Comparing the test scores for employees before and after training.

Answer Explanations

1. A: Minitab and Stata are examples of statistical software packages that allow the user to run statistical analyses and create statistical reports from inputted data sets. They're not spreadsheet specific software or statistical theorems. While these software packages make statistical calculations easier, they don't automate the process, as an operator is still needed to input data sets and decide which techniques should be performed for each individual data set.

2. C: Two-tail test. A two-tail test, also referred to as a non-directional hypothesis, tests the variables for relationships in either direction. With a two-tail test, the alpha error is divided into two equal parts at both tails of the distribution when testing for statistical significance. For example, if .05 is the significance level, then $\alpha = .025$ in each tail of the distribution. Therefore, the possibility of a relationship is being tested for in both directions.

3. A: This vector indicates linear relationships of positive notation. A negative relationship would show points traveling from the top-left of the graph to the bottom-right. Exponential and logarithmic functions aren't linear, so these options could have been immediately eliminated.

4. B: Correlation coefficients can range from -1, the strongest possible negative relationship, to 1, the strongest possible positive relationship. A correlation coefficient of 0 indicates no relationship. Even a correlation coefficient of 1 doesn't indicate causation, just a very strong correlation. A correlation coefficient of 1 always indicates a linear relationship. These details can eliminate the other answer choices.

5. C: A lowercase r indicates that this correlation coefficient describes the relationship between one predictor variable and one dependent variable. An uppercase R indicates that this correlation coefficient describes the relationship between multiple predictor variables and a dependent variable. The other options provided include some symbols that may be used in statistical analyses, but also include symbols that are illogical in this context.

6. D: Multicollinearity describes when two or more predictor variables may have a significant relationship with the outcome being studied, and it's difficult to tell which predictor variable is influencing the outcome. Multicollinearity typically takes place within multiple regression analyses, but not all multiple regression analyses experience this phenomenon. Statistical noise and significant confusion are not standard terms.

7. D: When a data set plots as a non-linear shape, this means that a relationship exists between the predictor and dependent variables. However, a linear regression technique doesn't help to explain the relationship. A line that travels from the top-left of a graph to the bottom-right of a graph indicates a negative/inverse relationship between the variables. If a line exists, but data points are also found outside of the line shape, those points are referred to as outliers. Finally, a line that travels from the bottom-left of a graph to the upper-right of a graph indicates a positive/direct relationship between the variables.

8. B: Cyclical variation is also referred to as part-to-part or lot-to-lot variation, and tracks variations from unit to unit. Temporal variation is also referred to as shift-to-shift variation, and tracks time-related variations. Positional variation is also referred to as within-part variation, and looks at characteristics on individual units or products. Product-to-product variation is not a common term for any type of variation.

9. C: Paired *t*-test. The paired *t*-test matches each data point in one sample with a data point in another sample to determine the difference. Therefore, equal sample sizes are necessary. The one-way ANOVA compares the means of three or more samples and doesn't require equal sample sizes. The two-sample proportion test also doesn't require equal sample sizes.

10. D: None of the above. On a multi-variate line chart, the plots located on and comprising the length of each vertical line represent variations within the samples. Variations from sample to sample, however, are represented by the position of the vertical lines. The graph is constructed by placing the time scale along the horizontal axis and the values along the vertical axis.

11. A: One-sample proportion test. A one-sample proportion test can determine if the proportion of a sample set is significantly different from a given proportion of its population. The two-sample proportion test is used for proportions of two independent samplings. The paired *t*-test and one-sample *t*-test are methods for determining differences in the means of sample sets.

12. C: Type I Error occurs when the null hypothesis is incorrectly rejected. For example, if products were considered defective when they were actually non-defective, this is Type I Error. Type I Errors are also referred to as false positives, alpha (α) errors, or alpha risk.

13. A: Type II Error occurs when the null hypothesis isn't rejected when it should have been. If products were considered non-defective when they were actually defective, this is a Type II Error. Type II Errors are also referred to as false negatives, beta (β) errors, or beta risk. Type I errors occur when the null hypothesis should have been accepted, but is rejected.

14. B: Statistically significant. Statistical significance translates to rejecting the null hypothesis; in other words, it correlates to the probability of a relationship existing between the variables and samples rather than being due to sampling error or chance. Statistical significance is represented by the p-value. P-value is the probability that the test statistic is equal to or less than the significance level. If the p-value is less than the significance level, then the test is considered statistically significant.

15. A: Compare the marital status of adults of different ethnic groups. The chi-square test for a contingency table can determine whether there is a difference between the distributions of two categorical variables. A categorical variable produces an assigned category as its outcome. The only scenario involving two categorical variables is Choice *A*. Choices *B*, *C*, and *D* all involve continuous variables (used for measurement).

Improve Phase

This section discusses how to maintain and sustain process and quality improvements after implementing a change in operations. The control phase is the final phase of an improvement process, although it's considered an ongoing, continuous phase.

Design of Experiments (DOE)

Basic Terms

Independent and dependent variables are used to solve problems and improve processes. When designing an experiment, the goal is to determine a cause and effect relationship between these two types of variables.

Independent variables represent causes or inputs, which are also known as *factors*. These variables are not affected by changes to the dependent variable(s). They are manipulated during an experiment to cause a change to the output(s) or dependent variable(s). Examples of independent variables include hours of tutoring and hours of marathon training.

Dependent variables represent the outcomes or outputs, which are also known as *responses*. These are the variables that "depend" on and are affected by the independent variable(s). They are measured during the experiment. Examples of dependent variables include scores on SAT exams and placements in the New York City Marathon.

Experiments are conducted at levels (or different factor values), and a combination of the levels of the factors that are being investigated is involved in each run of an experiment. Each combination is referred to as a *treatment*. A full factorial design is a design where every setting of every factor is present with every setting of every other factor. For example, an experiment with full factorial design that has three inputs or factors each taking two levels will have eight combinations ($2^3 = 8$). DOE has termed this as a 2x3 factorial design. Fractional factorial designs are also used for experiments when it is not practical to screen all of the inputs due to concerns with time and/or cost.

When changes are made to a factor's (input's) settings that result in a change to the response, it is known as an *effect*. The main effect is a term used for the effect of a single factor.

The order in which the trials of an experiment are conducted in is known as *randomization*. The effects of uncontrolled and unknown variables can be reduced or eliminated by using a randomized sequence. Randomization can also assist with helping to minimize or avoid any potential uncontrolled biases.

When randomization is not feasible, *blocking* is a technique that allows the individual conducting an experiment to run all of the trials using one setting of a factor and then run all of the trials again using a different setting of that factor. Thus, this tactic restricts randomization. Examples could involve running an experiment by isolating different lots of a raw material or isolating different shifts.

Repetition involves repeating an experiment before moving onto another combination and changing the conditions. On the other hand, replication occurs when the entire set of combinations is repeated after all of the runs are finished. *Replication* is more costly since it involves additional trials. However, it allows for the individual running the study to investigate interactions from the original trials. Experimentation error can also be estimated.

Any unexplained variations from observations that have been collected are referred to as errors. There are two types of errors: random errors and lack of fit errors. Random errors are also known as experimental errors and occur due to natural variations in the process. An example may involve an individual failing to read the measurement of a quantity properly because he or she has to estimate between fine lines on an instrument. Lack of fit errors result from deficiencies in the model itself.

DOE Graphs and Plots

For the experiment that is represented in the table below, the first factor is lack of sleep. Participants in the study are deprived of sleep for a period of either 2 hours or 18 hours. The second factor is type of supplement. Participants in the study are given an energy drink or a placebo drink.

Effect of lack of sleep & energy drinks on final exam scores

1) Lack of sleep
   a. 2 hours
   b. 18 hours

2) Type of supplement
   a. Energy drink
   b. Placebo drink

The X-axis would represent the lack of sleep (with 2 hours and 18 hours as tick marks), and the Y-axis would represent the participants' final exam scores (with 0 to 100 as tick marks). The lines that would appear in the middle of the chart would represent the data from the groups of participants who received the two types of supplements (energy drinks or placebo drinks).

The first step in the process is to perform *main effects analysis*. To determine if there is a main effect of lack of sleep, the data from the groups of participants who received the two types of supplements is ignored. The interest lies in finding out if there is a difference in the average performance between the participants who experienced a lack of sleep of 2 hours versus 18 hours. In order to determine that, the average between the energy drink and placebo drink groups must be calculated at 2 hours and 18 hours. The points representing the two averages are plotted to see if they are indeed different. In this example, the points are different. In a similar manner, to determine if there is a main effect of type of supplement, the data from the participants who experienced lack of sleep in the 2 hour and 18 hour groups is ignored. The interest lies in finding out if there is a difference in the average performance between the participants who was given energy drinks versus placebo drinks. In order to determine that, the average performance is calculated for the energy drink and placebo drink groups (roughly the middle of each line). The points representing the two averages are plotted to see if they are indeed different. In this example, the points are different.

The next step in the process is to determine if there is an *interaction* between the two factors, which means that one factor affects the performance of the second factor. In order to determine this, the difference in the group of participants that received energy drinks between the 2 hour and 18 hour marks is calculated (about 15%). Then the difference in the group of participants that received placebo drinks between the 2 hour and 18 hour marks is calculated (about 65%). The next step is to determine if the difference of 15 (from the energy drink) is different than the difference of 65 (from the lack of sleep). The performance of the participants who received the placebo drinks deteriorated significantly after they experienced a lack of sleep of 18 hours. The performance of the participants who received the energy drinks still dropped off after they experienced a lack of sleep of 18 hours, but not as severely.

Thus, one can conclude there is an interaction, which means that energy drinks are helping to alleviate the effects of sleep deprivation.

Root Cause Analysis

A problem solving method that is used to identify the root cause of a problem or key points of failure is *root cause analysis (RCA)*. The general steps to be taken in root cause analysis are as follows:

- Define the problem requiring analysis
- Understand the problem
- Collect data to analyze
- Determine the root cause or causes
- Create a corrective action plan
- Implement the action plan that was created
- Evaluate the implementation to see if the problem was solved

There are many tools that can be used to help identify the true cause of a problem.

Brainstorming is a simple method that is used to generate a large number of ideas in a relatively short period of time. The necessary individuals are gathered together. Once the topic of the brainstorming session is reviewed, the participants are asked to share their ideas while a recorder takes summarized notes on a flipchart. As participants share, there is no criticism, discussion, or evaluation of ideas.

Affinity diagrams can be helpful when organizing information following a brainstorming session. When creating an affinity diagram, individual ideas are recorded on sticky notes that are placed on a large table. Participants work to rearrange the sticky notes that contain ideas which are related in some way until all of the notes belong to smaller groups. Headings for the various groups that capture the overall meaning of the ideas contained within the groups are then determined by the participants.

Multi-voting can also be used following a brainstorming session to narrow down a large list of possibilities. The list of options is presented on a whiteboard. Each participant is given slips of paper that associate to a specific number of votes (typically 5 to 10, depending on the size of the list). Each participant works individually to select the five items he or she feels is most important and writes the choices on separate slips of papers with the associated rankings next to them. The slips of paper are collected, and the votes are tallied. The rankings that the items received are written on the whiteboard.

Kaoru Ishikawa is best known for his fishbone, or cause and effect, diagram that can be used to brainstorm all of the possible causes of a problem in order to sort ideas into categories that will ultimately lead to a solution. The causes can be grouped into various categories (people, methods, machines, materials, measurements, and environment) for the purpose of identifying the sources of variation. When participants are working on developing a fishbone diagram, it is important for them to focus on the causes instead of possible solutions and to keep asking "why" until it no longer makes sense to continue.

A Pareto chart is an important Six Sigma project tool that consists of a vertical bar graph with independent variables shown on the X-axis and dependent variables shown as the heights of the bars. The values on the graph are shown from left to right in a decreasing order of relative frequency. This type of chart is very helpful in pointing out the problems that need to be addressed first by a project team.

Lean Tools

Lean is a methodology with roots in Japanese manufacturing. Lean's concepts and methodologies were initially developed by Toyota Motor Corporation and focus on system-wide process and quality improvements. In turn, these improvements conserve valuable resources through small operational changes. Lean adopted many ideologies from just-in-time manufacturing concepts, which aim to reduce processing times in the manufacturing space while increasing pick-up time from the marketplace.

Waste Elimination

Lean systems are able to maximize production and/or service while minimizing the use of non-financial resources. These controls normally focus on how to most efficiently utilize manpower, materials, space, etc. Most organizations develop unique systems of utilizing lean principles based on methodologies most applicable to their products, services, and work environments. Regardless of the approach, the primary objective is to reduce waste (or *muda*, in the original Japanese philosophy) in seven areas. These are:

- Defects, or product issues that would lead a client to return a finished product
- Overproduction, or producing a greater quantity of a product than demand
- Transportation, or the need to physically move a product
- Wait, or any time when employees or consumers are waiting for something related to a product or service
- Inventory, or materials that aren't actively creating capital for the organization
- Motion, or the physical labor performed by employees and/or equipment
- Over-processing, or adding features to products or training to employees that aren't essential or fail to add value for the client/company

Lean controls are guided by basic principles examined and documented by James P. Womack, Daniel Roos, and Daniel T. Jones in *The Machine That Changed the World* (1990) and again by Womack and Jones in *Lean Thinking (1996)*. These principles include:

- Defining value from the customer's perspective and shaping processes to create a service or product that delivers this value. This principle usually takes into account features of the product or service, its availability, and its cost to the client or customer. A key factor in defining the value of a product or service is how well it fits a need as specified by the customer or client.

- Noticing which operational processes add value in creating the finished product, and if any operational processes that fail to add value can be removed from the process flow.

- Sequentially organizing necessary, value-adding process flow components in the most efficient manner based on the work environment.

- Finding a workflow balance that matches product supply to customer demand.

- Continuously examining and improving processes and acknowledging there's always room for improvement in operations. Continuous improvement is also commonly referred to by the Japanese term kaizen in professional organizations.

Pull Systems

Pull systems use production scheduling to avoid excessive inventory and create a more rapid delivery process. Materials and resources are only moved into the manufacturing process when customer sales necessitate more production. Only the amount that is needed to meet demand is produced which limits overproduction. Minimizing setup time, eliminating steps and rework, managing bottlenecks, and positioning of inventory are all aspects of a pull system.

Control Methods for 5S

5S is another process improvement methodology that aims to streamline operational processes. This system uses lean principles while incorporating methods to standardize, organize, and optimize an organization's practices and standard of cleanliness. These aspects also contribute to overall workplace and occupational safety for employees.

5S was originally a Japanese tool consisting of five words beginning with the letter S. The American adoption of this system also includes five English words that begin with S. The Japanese and English terms of the 5S process improvement methodology are:

- Seiri/Sort: Sort, or remove, materials not physically needed for the tasks at hand. Remove unnecessary clutter that can contribute to a hazardous working environment, employee distraction or confusion, and overall waste. Prevent items that aren't needed for the process at hand from entering the workspace.

- Seiton/Set: Set up materials that are necessary and valuable to the operational process flow. Organize them in an efficient, sequential, and logical manner. Keep process materials close to the operator.

- Seiso/Shine: Keep the work space clean, disinfected, and free of dirt (or "shiny"). Perform routine and thorough maintenance of equipment.

- Seiketsu/Standardize: Standardize processes to keep the workplace clean, organized, and efficient so all units and employees are able to contribute easily. Develop, advertise, and utilize best practices.

- Shitsuke/Sustain: Sustain the practices of efficiency, organization, and cleanliness by habitually revisiting organizational processes that contribute to high-level functioning and workplace safety.

Some organizations add an additional S for safety, and refer to this system as *6S*. Many argue that the additional S is unnecessary, as safety should be inherent and prioritized within each facet of the 5S system.

Kanban

Kanban is a Japanese term that means "sign" or "billboard." The Kanban system focuses on scheduling tasks in an operational process to control inventory and streamline manufacturing and the supply chain. A Kanban system almost always uses a board, or cards on a board, as a visual aid to illustrate process flow. The system may use colored cards, or some other visual feature, to indicate priority level, team assignment, deadline, or other components of the tasks at hand. Tasks of the operational process will be organized on the board to depict responsibilities to be completed, tasks in process, completed tasks, and any issues that may arise. A comprehensive Kanban system plays a pivotal role in continuous improvement, as it can establish efficient processes, uncover problematic processes, indicate important baseline and outcome metrics (timing, cost, resource utilization, etc.), and be continuously updated.

While Kanban systems were originally displayed on physical white boards, contemporary Kanban systems may be virtual. Virtual Kanban boards are necessary for teams that work remotely. Virtual boards are able to work in conjunction with email, auditing, project management, and metric-tracking software, which increases overall organizational efficiency.

Poka-Yoke (Mistake Proofing)

Poka-yoke comes from the Japanese words *poka*, meaning mistake, and *yokeru*, meaning avoid. Poka-yoke is a construct of lean that focuses on minimizing or eliminating mistakes, especially human mistakes (as opposed to machine or software errors). Like Kanban, poka-yoke tools tend to be visual. Poka-yoke is regarded as the first step in preventing errors across a workflow process. Error-proofing is an important component of manufacturing processes, with the goal of designing a process so fail-proof that it cannot be performed incorrectly. Three specific methodologies are used in manufacturing systems to prevent errors:

- Contact Method: Examines and tests the physical characteristics of a product, such as its shape and size.
- Fixed-Value Method: Examines product movement.
- Motion-Step Method: Examines the sequence of operations.

The following principles guide poka-yoke techniques:

- Implementing rules and concrete operating procedures that prevent the creation of defects.
- Preventing defective materials, parts, or products from progressing into a subsequent stage of the production process.
- Utilizing warning systems to indicate the presence of errors.

An important distinction in the poka-yoke technique is the difference between defects and mistakes. Mistakes are believed to be statistically unavoidable, and poka-yoke aims to minimize the presence of mistakes as much as possible by reducing the presence of defects. Defects are problems that can be avoided or noted before the defective product ever reaches the marketplace.

The introduction of technology and software tools in the workplace is an example of poka-yoke techniques, as these often lead to automating processes previously performed by humans. However, software systems require their own poka-yoke controls, which has introduced a new dimension to the methodology.

Standard Work

Standard work refers to the process of establishing a baseline which represents the "best practices" of how a product or part is produced. Every step in a production process is performed repeatedly to identify the most efficient sequencing and usage of resources. The baseline can be used to compare to subsequent production runs to identify variances in an effort to continually improve the process. Standard work utilizes analysis and observation of both human motion and the interaction of humans and machines. Employees are a key resource in the process of developing baselines because they are the most involved with the work and the work process.

Cycle-time Reduction

In an effort to reduce cycle time, it is imperative to ensure a *continuous flow*. Continuous flow is accomplished when the creation of a service or product passes through a set of steps without experiencing any defects, delays, or operations that are non-valued added in nature during the production process.

In addition to shorter cycle times, some benefits of continuous flow include identifying and eliminating bottlenecks, increased throughput, and lower inventory levels. By improving the movement of information or material through a process, continuous flow ultimately eliminates waste. Reducing lot sizes and allowing for quick changeovers are some ways to improve flow.

The total amount of time from the last piece of a product made by a process to the first good piece of a product made by another process is known as setup time. The goal is to minimize the amount of setup time (which is non-value added time), so equipment will not be left idle and customers can be attended to in a timelier manner.

Setup reduction is also known as quick changeover or single minute exchange of dies (SMED). The first step in this methodology involves observing the current process and identifying whether setup activities are internal or external. Internal activities require that production be stopped (signifies lost time), and external activities can be performed while production is running. Examples of internal activities include clearing hoppers and removing guards from equipment. Examples of external activities include locating paperwork and obtaining tools or raw materials. The second step involves converting as many internal activities as possible to external activities. An example of this is to have an additional set of pre-cleaned, changeover parts available instead of having to clean and re-use the parts that are already in use. Since there are still some steps that cannot be performed while machines are operational, simplifying or reducing the time for the remaining internal activities is the third step in this process. Examples of this include using preset gauges and quick disconnect fittings for water, power, and air where possible. The final step in this process is to streamline the external activities. Examples of this include reorganizing a workspace to eliminate motion, standardizing hardware that is used so fewer tools are required, and storing documentation as close to the point of use as possible.

Single minute exchange of dies (SMED) is a continuous improvement process which can result in lower batch sizes, reduced inventory, increased capacity, higher equipment utilization, more flexibility, improved safety, and lower waiting times.

Kaizen and Kaizen Blitz

Kaizen is a Japanese term for continuous improvement. Kaizen focuses on planned, small, incremental changes to improve processes, which, in turn, will increase productivity and quality, while reducing waste. The thinking behind Kaizen is that many small improvements can lead to big results. Processes are monitored once changes are made. Then adjustments are implemented, if needed, in order to reach the desired results. Kaizen may be difficult to implement in organizations that utilize a top-down approach, since the process encourages experimentation and input from employees.

Some examples of successful implementation of Kaizen include: a bank that decreased the number of steps for a customer to open a new checking account, an office furniture company that significantly increased productivity and was able to produce its most popular office chair in mere seconds, and a hospital system that worked on its internal processes which resulted in lowering the amount of money spent on ordering office supplies.

A *kaizen blitz* is concerned with taking about a week to correct one specific issue. Since the focus of a kaizen blitz is narrower, it is used after improvements are already in the process of being made. It tends to be reactive in nature since it is used to fix a process after it is already broken.

A kaizen blitz is made up of three stages: a preparation stage, the blitz event itself, and a follow-up stage. During the preparation stage, it is imperative to have a sponsor from senior management. The scope of the problem to be addressed during the blitz is defined, along with the associated improvements that are being sought. All data and necessary process information that will need to be available to the team during the blitz is gathered. The blitz team is chosen and briefed.

At the start of the blitz, team members participate in process training. A process map walk-through is conducted, and data is collected and analyzed. Possible solutions are discussed, refined, and prioritized. Solution implementation is started. A summary of the final analysis and solutions is prepared, along with an implementation plan. The summary is presented to the senior management sponsor and key stakeholders.

During the follow-up session, any implementation actions that were not completed during the blitz are worked on, process changes are communicated, and benefits and impacts are measured.

It is important to note that companies can misuse this technique by wanting to obtain quick-fixes and then being disappointed because the problems were deep-rooted and systemic issues were not properly addressed. Companies may choose to utilize a kaizen blitz when they are interested in eliminating work in progress or reducing floor space, inventory, and/or set-up time.

Practice Questions

1. The concept of lean manufacturing was originally developed and introduced by which of the following organizations?
    a. Toyota Motor Corporation
    b. Stanford University
    c. Silicon Valley
    d. Motorola

2. Marcy is a manufacturing engineer for a global company. She has to make multiple copies of protocols regularly for her lab, so she walks to the copier almost hourly. The copier is located on the other side of her large building. This process is wasteful in terms of which aspect of lean methodology?
    a. Defects
    b. Inventory
    c. Motion
    d. Transportation

3. In English, the 5S system stands for which of the following terms?
    a. Standardize, Simplify, Sell, Sort, Snap
    b. Sort, Set, Shine, Standardize, Sustain
    c. Sort, Sell, Stream, Safe, Supply
    d. Supply, Sell, Sustain, Seal, Simple

4. Joe holds a continuous improvement event for his manufacturing team to streamline an existing process. For some reason, his team produces too many units. He brings in a whiteboard and different colored cards to signify each component of the process as they occur. He divides the board into rows to show what happens before production, during production, and after production. Joe is using which of the following tools to help his team?
    a. Kanban
    b. Poka-yoke
    c. Kaizen
    d. Muda

5. Which of the following is an example of an independent variable?
    a. Scores on an exam
    b. Hours of studying
    c. Placements in a race
    d. A drug's impact on a disease

6. A DOE that is termed 2x4 has how many combinations of the levels of the factors that are being investigated?
    a. 8
    b. 6
    c. 16
    d. 4

7. When changes are made to a factor's settings that result in a change to the response, it is known as which of the following?
   a. Effect
   b. Level
   c. Randomization
   d. Factorial

8. Which of the following terms means the entire set of combinations is repeated after all of the runs are finished?
   a. Randomization
   b. Repetition
   c. Random errors
   d. Replication

9. In DOE, the effect that an independent variable has on a dependent variable averaging across the levels of any other independent variables is known as which of the following?
   a. Interaction effect
   b. Main effect
   c. Factorial design
   d. Experiment

10. In DOE, if one factor is proven to affect the performance of a second factor, it is known as which of the following?
    a. Main effect
    b. Experiment
    c. Interaction effect
    d. Factorial design

11. Which of the following is an example of a dependent variable?
    a. Amount of liquid absorbed by a paper towel
    b. Absence of caffeine
    c. Brand of paper towel
    d. Presence of caffeine

12. Which of the following is a method used to assist with root cause analysis?
    a. SMED
    b. Kaizen blitz
    c. TPM
    d. Brainstorming

13. Which of the following is NOT a benefit of continuous flow?
    a. Less bottlenecks
    b. Higher inventory levels
    c. Increased throughput
    d. Shorter cycle time

14. The total amount of time from the last piece of a product made by a process to the first good piece of a product made by another process is known as which of the following?
    a. Setup reduction
    b. Continuous flow
    c. Setup time
    d. SMED

15. Which of the following is the major difference between a Kaizen blitz and Kaizen?
    a. A Kaizen blitz focuses on correcting one issue, while Kaizen focuses on small changes to improve processes.
    b. A Kaizen blitz does not encourage employee contributions, and Kaizen does.
    c. A Kaizen blitz is made up of three stages, while Kaizen is made up of twenty steps.
    d. There really is no major difference between Kaizen and a Kaizen blitz.

Answer Explanations

1. A: Toyota Motor Corporation developed Lean from just-in-time manufacturing principles to conserve valuable resources through small operational changes. Lean systems describe systems that are able to maximize production while minimizing the amount of non-financial, valuable resources used. The other organizations mentioned are not known for developing Lean methodologies.

2. C: Motion includes waste related to employee effort and movement. Marcy could be more efficient if the copy machine was located near her workspace, or if she made all of her copies at one time during the day. Defects refer to defective products that have to be trashed rather than sold, so all the work and material that went into making the products is considered waste. Inventory refers to having more product than what can sell, leading to waste of material, labor, and storage. Transportation refers to any time a product has to be moved from one place to another. These options aren't relevant to the example in the question.

3. B: Sort, Set, Shine, Standardize, and Sustain define a system intended to help organizations standardize, organize, and optimize its practices and standard of cleanliness. These aspects also contribute to overall workplace and occupational safety for employees. The other options don't include all of these components.

4. A: A Kanban system almost always uses a board, or cards on a board, as a visual aid to illustrate process flow. This system focuses on scheduling tasks in an operational process to control inventory and streamline the manufacturing and supply chain. Poka-yoke refers to mistake proofing, and is not relevant. Kaizen is a term meaning continuous improvement, and is a very broad concept. Muda refers to all waste. While Joe is trying to eliminate waste, the question asks about a specific tool Joe is using that is defined by a whiteboard and colored cards.

5. B: Hours of studying is an example of an independent variable. In this example, hours of studying is an input that will not be affected by changes to a dependent variable, such as a score on an exam. The remaining answer choices are all examples of dependent variables.

6. C: A DOE that is termed 2x4 has 16 possible combinations of the levels of the factors that are being investigated since 2x4 is representative of (2^4=16).

7. A: When changes are made to a factor's setting that result in a change to the response, it is known as effect. Levels are the settings for each factor in an experiment, such as temperature. Conducting experimental runs in no particular order is known as randomization. Finally, factorial is referring to a full factorial design where the response of all possible combinations of factors and factor levels are measured in order to provide information about main effects and interaction effects.

8. D: Replication takes place when the entire set of combinations is repeated after all of the runs are finished. Conducting experimental runs in no particular order is known as randomization. Repetition in DOE utilizes the same subjects with every condition of the research. Finally, random errors are caused by unpredictable and unknown changes in an experiment.

9. B: Main effect is the effect that an independent variable has on a dependent variable averaging across the levels of any other independent variables in DoE. An interaction effect is present in DOE when the effect of one of the factors is dependent upon the level of a second factor. Factorial design is referring to a full factorial design where the response of all possible combinations of factors and factor levels are measured in order to provide information about main effects and interaction effects. Finally, an experiment is set up to test a hypothesis.

10. C: Interaction effect is when one factor is proven to affect the performance of a second factor in DoE. A main effect is present in DOE when different levels of a factor are shown to affect the response differently. An experiment is set up to test a hypothesis. Finally, factorial design is referring to a full factorial design where the response of all possible combinations of factors and factor levels are measured in order to provide information about main effects and interaction effects.

11. A: The amount of liquid that is absorbed by a paper towel is an example of a dependent variable. In this example, the amount of liquid absorbed is an outcome which would be affected by changes to an independent variable, such as the brand of paper towel used. The remaining answer choices are all examples of independent variables.

12. D: Brainstorming is a method used to assist with root cause analysis. SMED is a tool used to assist with cycle-time reduction. Kaizen blitz is a focused and intensive approach to process improvement. Finally, TPM is a process for improving equipment effectiveness.

13. B: Lower inventory levels is a benefit of continuous flow. Together with decreased bottlenecks, increased throughput, and shorter cycle time these benefits help to eliminate waste in a process by improving movement and flow within the process.

14. C: Setup time is the total amount of time from the last piece of a product made by a process to the first good piece of a product made by another process. Setup reduction is an important technique that can significantly reduce the amount of time that it takes to switch from producing one type of product to another. This is also commonly referred to as single minute exchange of dies or SMED. Continuous flow simply means that the flow of value-add does not cease. An ideal process continues to add value without ceasing during the entire production process.

15. A: The major difference between a Kaizen blitz and Kaizen is the fact that a Kaizen blitz is designed to rapidly produce results for a process issue within a few days, while Kaizen is more of an ongoing philosophy of continuous improvement.

Control Phase

Statistical Process Control (SPC)

Statistical process control (SPC) is a systematic, data-centered process that drives continuous quality improvement. This methodology uses real-time data from quality-related processes in the organization's workflow (the data may be derived directly from quantifiable aspects of the finished product). SPC was first developed in the 1920s by Walter A. Shewhart, who later wrote the acclaimed *Statistical Method from the Viewpoint of Quality Control* (1939). The overarching goal is to standardize the workflow process by eliminating variation. SPC utilizes upper and lower control limits to catch process problems as they occur, rather than relying solely on inspection of the final product or service. Control limits are established depending on the specific process. They differ from *specification limits*, which refer to the parameters of the final product (make, size, quantity, and other attributes usually determined by the customer or marketplace). The benefits of SPC include reducing variability early in the process, implementing change as soon as an issue presents itself, increasing productivity, and overall cost savings.

SPC Basics

The SPC process makes use of a *control chart* (also known as a Shewhart chart). Control charts graph the evolution of a process change to determine if and how the change affects the operational process. Control charts monitor processes in order to catch problems before they become major issues, predict process outcomes, determine the reliability of an established process, and drive quality improvement projects. The emphasis that SPC places on detecting errors early in the process is one of its biggest advantages, as it helps with reducing overall waste along the entire workflow. Any variation is categorized into one of two groups: common causes and special causes. Common causes refer to normal instances of variation caused by routine, uncontrollable practices of the workflow (human employees who inherently work differently from one another although they follow the same set of standardized operating procedures). Special causes are abnormal and usually unpredictable instances of variation that are the direct result of non-routine circumstances (local power outage). While variation should be expected across all process flows, SPC aims to control variation as much as possible. While documented instances of variation may not be eliminated completely, parameters around variation may be implemented to limit frequency, range, etc. When variations have successfully been accounted for and limited, the overall process is considered to be "in control."

SPC has historically been used primarily in manufacturing settings. Due to the repetitive, predictable nature of manufacturing processes, SPC serves an ideal quality system. As technology becomes more widespread, SPC is also used to drive software and technological improvements. This is a controversial practice due to the non-repetitive nature of technological processes (software coding), and the rapid and constantly changing nature of the industry.

The starting point for SPC is to determine what type of data is desired. Data can be variable (usually referring to a continuous range of possible values, such as product weight), or attribute (usually discrete binary counts, such as pass/fail on an assembly line). An equally essential step is ensuring that data collection is as error-free as possible. A measurement system analysis (MSA) can be a crucial tool at this stage. The MSA will shape the quality of final data sets by setting guidelines for the data collection process. It's critical to have high-quality data sets if the results will be used to guide organizational and workflow decisions.

When collecting data, certain indicators of a robust measuring system are likely to limit variability:

- Stable: will provide the same results from an established sample set over time
- Accurate: collects correct and useful values
- Linearity: collects values at the same level of variation across samples
- Repeatability: a single operator can collect data multiple times from the same sample and obtain the same result each time
- Reproducibility: any operator can collect data from the same sample, and the same result will be obtained across different operators

A *Gage Repeatability and Reproducibility* (Gage R&R) Assessment worksheet provides comprehensive insight into how much variation in a data set is a result of user and measurement error. This assessment should be used as part of new employee onboarding, especially if the new employee will take any process measurements. These worksheets can be found for free online.

Once the data to be collected has been defined and the MSA has been completed, data collection can begin. Data should be collected at random. A determination should be made as to whether data should be collected between groups or within groups (i.e., if an assembly line changes shifts by time or process). The type and amount of data collected will determine how to chart the data, which is explained further in later sections. In general, data collected for SPC is visually depicted on one of the various control charts. These tools utilize upper, average, and lower limits to document process variation. When charting, it's important to document whether a unit was seen as nonconforming or defective during a process, why the issue occurred, and how the issue occurred. This information will help to guide process and quality improvement projects.

Rational Subgrouping

The practice of organizing data into groups of units produced under similar conditions is known as rational subgrouping. Subgroups are a reflection of how data is collected from a lone, stable process and are essentially a snapshot of that process during a moment in time (i.e., a short shift, a specific batch of output, etc.). Observations within the subgroups are independent of one another.

Two types of variation in a process can be separated by subgroups. The first type is variation between subgroups. This type of variation is the result of special causes or specific, identifiable factors. The second type of variation is within subgroup. This type of variation is the result of common causes and is represented on control charts. Dedicating time and thought behind a subgrouping strategy is extremely important so that the correct variation is displayed on a control chart in order to properly identify a process's source of variability.

In an example where a quality control inspector randomly selects and tests four parts at the top of every hour for a machine that produces fifty parts per hour, each sample of four parts is considered a subgroup.

In an example measuring quality in a situation where three machines are producing the same part, three different approaches to the subgrouping may include:

1. One sample taken from each of the three machines to form a subgroup of three each time

2. Three samples taken from the first machine make up the first subgroup, three samples taken from the second machine make up the second subgroup, and three samples taken from the third machine make up the final subgroup

3. Three samples taken from the blended production stream (from all of the machines) to form a subgroup of three each time

The best subgrouping plan would be the second option listed above since it minimizes the variation within each subgroup and maximizes the opportunity for variation to occur between the various subgroups. The other two options listed above cannot meet these two rules.

Control Charts

<u>I-MR Chart</u>
An *I-MR chart* is a control chart generally used to gauge the stability (control) of a process, indicate any potential issues that may cause instability, and illustrate whether tests of change resulted in any improvements or deficits. The "I" stands for "Individual," and the "MR" stands for "Moving Range."

An I-MR chart consists of two separate graphs. Individual, observed data values (I) are chronologically plotted on one graph, which is referred to as the I-chart. The I-chart examines overall process trends by way of these individual observations, so sequential ordering is essential. The second graph plots the variation, or moving range (MR) between one observed instance and the instance immediately following. This graph is referred to as the MR-chart. Upper and lower control limits are usually defined, but they're arbitrary points that don't have statistical significance, as they are generally limited to the process flow at hand. Data values plotted on I-MR charts aren't used for situations that may require repeatability or reproducibility. I-MR charts typically examine a very specific process flow within an organization. Points that fall outside of the established upper and lower control limits should be examined for special causes that may indicate a process that's out of control. Control limits for I-MR charts are easily calculated in almost all spreadsheet software or statistical software packages. Standard deviation isn't calculated from any data plotted on I-MR charts.

I-MR charts are typically used when group sizes are unknown or undefined. They are also used when data collection is time-consuming or laborious (when a complete manufacturing cycle takes a long time or is extraordinarily refined in nature, making observations limited in frequency).

<u>Xbar-R Chart</u>
X-bar & Range Charts (or X-bar & R Charts) are a common statistical process control procedure made up of two charts. These are optimal for contexts where the data type collected is continuous, the sample size is small and stable/consistent between groups (such as in batch manufacturing, where the process completes the same number of batches of products), and where the risk of human error is high (as this type of charting minimizes errors that can result from human calculation). X-bar charts plot the mean of each consecutive batch. R charts plot the range of consecutive sample groups. Together, these charts aim to show variation within groups.

R charts are considered somewhat outdated, and many organizations have substituted R charts with s charts, which plot the average standard deviation of consecutive sample groups. A general rule of thumb is to use R charts with sample sizes of eight or less and use s charts with sample sizes of nine or more. Whether using an R or s chart, the range or standard deviation shown establishes the upper and lower control limits. When using X-bar & R charts, the normal distribution around the mean is assumed for each sample group.

U Chart

U charts are part of statistical process control that depict groups larger than one which vary by size, and they typically focus on defects, anomalies, or other non-compliant instances of production. Examples include scratches or blemishes that may not indicate total product failure. Atypical production that doesn't lead to total product failure is known as nonconformity, where the product isn't necessarily defective, but it isn't produced to ideal specification. The data from U charts almost always skews to the right, as U charts follow Poisson distribution, a probability-focused distribution in modeling outcomes. Therefore, these data follow certain assumptions:

- The probability of observing a pre-determined event is proportional to the size of the interval
- The probability of two events occurring in a narrow interval are virtually non-existent
- The probability of an event occurring does not vary between intervals
- The probability of an event during an interval is independent of other interval events

U charts determine the stability of a process, and they can also be used to track process and quality improvement projects.

P Chart

In statistical process control, *p charts* also focus on defects, anomalies, and other non-compliant instances of production. Unlike u charts, p charts only apply to pass/fail contexts. There are no sample subgroups. Consequently, the data collected by p charts follow binomial distribution as well as these assumptions: the probability of the presence of a nonconformity is the same across all observations; all units are independent of each other; and the observation process doesn't vary between units. P charts determine the cause of variations and can also be used to shape process and quality improvement projects. Nonconforming units are later examined and expressed as a ratio to the rest of the sample. P charts are primarily used in contexts where there are only two possible outcomes, such as when monitoring ambulatory services, i.e. did the patient arrive to the emergency department in an ambulance or not.

NP Chart

NP charts track defects (an actual failed product). Defective products fail to meet specification limits, rather than control limits. Both control and specification limits are established at the beginning of documentation, the number of nonconforming units aren't later expressed as a ratio, and the sample size doesn't change. Like p charts, np charts follow binomial distributions. While p charts express nonconformities as a ratio or fraction, np charts express defects as a count.

X-S Chart

X-S control charts are similar to X-bar & R charts, but they use standard deviation (hence the S in the name) rather than range. X-S charts utilize two graphs. The X graph plots the mean of consecutive samples, and the S graph plots the standard deviation of consecutive samples. While X-bar & R charts work well with small sample sizes (generally eight or less), the range becomes a less accurate technique to account for variation with larger sample sizes. Some organizations may use them for all sample sizes, as standard deviation is a precise method for calculating variation. Standard deviation uses every data point available, as opposed to the range, which considers only the smallest and largest values.

<u>CUSUM Chart</u>
Unlike other control charts that monitor variation, cumulative sum (or *CUSUM*) charts focus on cumulative values, and can collect data values individually or by group. The mean will be calculated either by sample or across all individuals, and further statistics will be calculated from there. CUSUM charts assume normal data distributions.

Specifically, CUSUM charts plot the deviation of each observed value from what the value should actually be. This is a precise method that will pick up even small variations, and can detect changes usually defined by time (equipment calibration, personnel fatigue from beginning to end of shift, wear and tear on parts, etc.). CUSUM control charts are especially useful in ultra-refined contexts where even small data changes can cause notable outcome problems, and they work well with sample sizes of one.

<u>Control Chart Anatomy</u>
As illustrated by the preceding sections, a variety of control charts can track workflow processes in order to minimize nonconformities, defects, and variation. These charts also monitor process stability and causes of variation. While control charts vary in how they do so, all control charts usually include the following components:

- The variables or workflow aspects of interest, and how they act over time

- Observed values collected using a reliable and valid measuring system (data sample), plotted onto a graph

- The mean of the observed data, visually depicted as a thick, unbroken center line

- The variation of the observed data, including upper and lower control limits also visually depicted by parallel lines around the mean. When processes are in control, 99.7% of observed values should fall within these established control limits, assuming a normal distribution

- Outliers, which often signal cause for closer examination

- Patterns and trends over time from which the operator should be able to make forecasts and predictions

- Any site-specific notations which indicate points of interest for the unique workflow, operator, or organization at hand

Control Plan

A Six Sigma control plan is a crucial part of process planning. The control plan sets the foundation for a stable workflow, high-quality products and services, and strong organizational operations. A control plan is comprehensive, detailed documentation that establishes how the process should flow within certain specifications and expected outcomes and also details the steps to take if the process becomes out of control. The American Society for Quality recommends a systematic approach to developing a Six Sigma focused control plan. This approach suggests linearly documenting: the process description; those who receive value from the process; those who perform the process; the process steps; key performance indicators and associated measurements; needs and expectations of the process; control charts that will be used to monitor the process; corrective plans and how they will be implemented; a date log; and any other relevant information.

To this end, a control plan normally includes the following components:

- Measurements and specifications: Define what is to be measured in order to set a target rate (i.e. completion rate, completion time, product ability to withstand drops, etc.) and define what measurement levels indicate successful performance (i.e. defect rate, revenue, customer satisfaction surveys, etc.). Determine the key performance indicators (KPIs) for the process.

- Inputs and outputs: Document the components that enter the process and when/what should result from their input.

- Process design and execution: Detail how and why the process was created and exact steps to be followed (this could provide adequate instruction to any operator).

- Frequency of reporting and sampling: Document how often process outputs will be sampled, what details will be obtained, and how those details will be noted. Have a standard process and format for reporting.

- Recording: Document as much as possible from assessment to output. Use standard forms for processes to allow data to be easily gleaned.

- Corrective actions: Include a comprehensive, logical, and systematic method for fixing problems, including the definition of what constitutes an error in the process.

- Process owner: Appoint a person or group responsible for overseeing the process and the control plan, including the ability to make final decisions.

Control plans may also include flowcharts, specifications, standard operating procedures, and any other miscellaneous material pertinent to the process.

Elements of the Control Plan

Control plans are living documents that can be modified as needed in order for them to remain useful to the process members and effective as monitoring tools. After a process owner is established, he or she is responsible for ensuring the control plan is followed and updated as needed. Elements to the control plan can include the following:

- History of the process
- History of the team members involved in the process
- Trainings or additional education needed and completed by team members
- Materials and resources needed
- Customers or clients of the process
- Value stream of the process
- Proof of concept
- Flow charts (a series of descriptions and decision points that guide the process flow)
- Input and output variables
- Data collection and management details (i.e. sample sizes, measurement technique, storage)
- Statistics needed and produced

- Failures
- Corrective action process flow and documentation
- Tests of change
- Outcomes needed and expected
- Standard forms that are used to collect data, monitor data, track changes, or create reports
- Specifications

Control plans will also utilize standard formatting and organizational conventions, such as:

- Plan name
- Plan number
- Page numbers
- Version number
- Revision history
- Author(s)

Elements of the Response Plan

A control plan sets boundaries within which the process should operate. *Response plans* address instances where change is needed. When observed values from the process fall outside of these boundaries (go out of control), a response is needed. This could be in response to an error, inefficiency, some other event that necessitates corrective action, or as a means to support preventative action steps (which is ideal). A response plan includes the following:

- Definitions of contexts that require a response or intervention
- A process to troubleshoot errors, issues, and mistakes
- A process to fix errors, issues, and mistakes (often provided in the form of training manuals, guides, etc.)
- The length of time a response should take, and how long it should last (this will vary by process, team, and organization)
- Owners responsible for responding

A comprehensive response plan will ideally provide instructions to remedy the situation in the short-term to stop the ineffectual process and prevent similar actions from occurring in the long term. Response plans can take place in the following ways:

- Continue the current process to determine where the ineffective or dysfunctional processing occurs. This response is simply the first step to fixing the underlying causes of the issue and shouldn't be a terminal step.

- Override the process without making the situation worse (i.e., by implementing an alternative process that has not yet been proven to work).

- Determine what, if any, procedures exist in handling the ineffective or dysfunctional process.

- Determine if someone with higher authority or knowledge can manage the issue.

- "Stop, correct, resume" – a systematic approach that recommends stopping the entire process, correcting the issues, and resuming operations; while this is a thorough response, it may not provide an immediate solution.

Lean Tools for Process Control

Total Productive Maintenance (TPM)

A lean manufacturing tool that seeks to involve all employees in order to achieve maximum equipment effectiveness is known as total productive maintenance (TPM). This approach encourages employees to treat workplace equipment as their own. The focus of TPM is on increasing the effectiveness and stability of machines in order to combat the known six big losses of production shown in the graphic below.

Breakdown of machines
- Motors breaking down
- Fan belts breaking

Minor adjustments and setup losses
- Shortages in material
- Changeovers

Minor stoppages and idling
- Machine jams
- Inspections

Reduced speed
- Issues with incorrect alignments or settings

Startup losses
- Scrap
- Rework

Defects and rework
- Scrap
- Rework

The three goals of TPM are to have zero accidents, zero unplanned failures, and zero product defects. This is accomplished by implementing the eight pillars of TPM, which were developed by Seiichi Nakajima of the Japan Institute of Plant Maintenance (JIPM).

The first pillar of TPM is autonomous maintenance. Machine operators are responsible for performing both preventative and routine maintenance on the pieces of equipment that they work with on a daily basis. Individuals on the maintenance staff then have the necessary time to take care of more complex maintenance tasks. This allows the machine operators to gain more knowledge about and take greater ownership of their equipment. The machine operators are also better able to identify problems before they turn into major equipment breakdowns.

Planned maintenance is the second pillar of TPM. This involves scheduling maintenance activities based on observed breakdowns and/or failure rates, which can lead to machines having a longer service life. This type of maintenance can be scheduled so as not to interfere with when equipment is scheduled for production.

The third pillar of TPM is quality integration which focuses on equipment's ability to detect and prevent errors in order to produce a high quality product the first time. This, in turn, reduces the amount of rework that may need to take place. Thus, a reduction in cost results from the early detection of defects versus relying on an inspection process that may take place later in the process.

Focused improvement is the fourth pillar of TPM. Cross-functional teams are assembled for the purpose of proactively identifying problematic equipment and/or recurring problems that they can work together to develop creative solutions for as part of a continuous improvement effort.

The fifth pillar of TPM is early equipment management. The goal is for new machinery to reach its optimal performance levels much faster. This is due to the experience obtained from prior maintenance improvement activities which will be factored into the design of the new equipment through input by employees. There should also be less startup issues, as employees will also be involved with the installation of the new equipment. Therefore, the overall maintenance costs of new equipment will be reduced.

Education and training is the sixth pillar of TPM. Employee training (managers, operators, and maintenance personnel) in Total Productive Maintenance (TPM) is essential to ensure that no knowledge gaps exist throughout the organization in order for the TPM goals to be attained.

The seventh pillar of TPM is health, safety, and environment. This pillar involves providing a safe environment for workers to allow them to be able to perform their daily job functions without risk to their health and well-being. The ultimate goal is to have a workplace that is accident-free.

TPM in office functions is the eighth and final pillar which focuses on applying the techniques of Total Productive Maintenance to address any waste in administrative functions. This, in turn, supports the production process through the use of improved office functions, such as scheduling and procurement.

There are several benefits to using TPM. This approach will improve the uptime of equipment which will save an organization money. TPM can also help to prolong the life of equipment. In addition, the teamwork between maintenance personnel and machine operators will improve.

Visual Factory

An approach to a lean manufacturing environment where visual information is conveyed about data and information throughout the workplace is known as a visual factory. This is accomplished through charts, signs, photographs, labels, electrical display boards, and dashboards. The goal of a visual factory is to allow all employees to visualize the tasks inside of a company and to increase the speed of information transmission. Resources and time that are spent communicating information more than once or in more than one type of medium are looked upon as being wasteful. Employees are able to spend less time reading text-based instructions in a visual factory. For example, instead of the need to read through formal work instructions, employees can refer to flow charts and work samples instead. The first step in creating a visual factory is to decide on the information that needs to be conveyed. Then how to best share the information must be determined.

The creation of a visual factory in many organizations goes hand in hand with the implementation of a 5S program, which is also part of Kaizan and focuses on visual order in the workplace. The first "S" in the system stands for the Japanese word Seiri, which translates to the English word Sort. This step deals with removing any unnecessary items from the workplace, which involves removing clutter from the items that are actually needed to perform a particular process. The Japanese word Seiton, which translates to the English phrase Set In Order is the second "S" in the system. The phrase "a place for everything and everything in its place" defines this step, which involves creating specific locations for everything. Using ergonomic principles, all of the required items for a process are arranged in the most efficient manner. The third "S" in the system stands for the Japanese word Seiso, which translates to the English word Shine. This step involves making everything appear new in in the work area by thoroughly cleaning all of the equipment, machines, and tools. By doing so, any non-conformities will become clearly noticeable, such as machine oil leaks. The Japanese word Seiketsu, which translates to the English word Standardize is the fourth "S" in the system. The focus during this step is on standardizing best practices in the workplace, such as institutionalizing the first three steps that have been performed in the process. This fifth and final "S" in the system stands for the Japanese word Shitsuke, which translates to the English word Sustain. Since employees want to ensure that they never slip back into their old ways, this step is concerned with maintenance housekeeping, conducting audits, and continuous improvement. It is important to remember that the responsibility for a successful 5S program belongs to all parties within a company.

There are numerous benefits to a lean manufacturing environment implementing a visual factory. A visual factory leads to a safer workplace. This occurs by visually identifying hazards and safe areas. For example, by strategically marking floor paths, aisles, and exits, as well as providing wayfinding signage, employees are better able to navigate their surroundings. A decrease in errors results from a visual factory. There is less guesswork on the part of the employees when photographs and graphics provide them with clear and concise instructions on how to perform a process. This is a much more effective method than employees receiving verbal or long, written descriptions that can be interpreted in numerous different ways. Thus, employees have a greater overall sense of confidence about their work. Additionally, output is increased and productivity is improved through the use of a visual factory. Machines are used in the most efficient manner, which results in improvements in the amount of time they are operational, along with increased run rates. Work also stays in progress for a less amount of time. A visual factory also leads to higher profits. This is due to the fact that the processes in the workplace have been reorganized to be more efficient in nature.

Practice Questions

1. Sandbag Company is a small business that fills sandbags for coastal homeowners to use during tropical storms and hurricanes. The Operations Supervisor is in charge of tracking the amount of sand filled in each bag by the company's sand distributing equipment. He normally uses X-S charts to track the weight of each bag, and groups the samples by 20. However, he could also monitor the process by doing which of the following?
    a. Grouping the samples by 5 and using X-bar & R charts to track variations in weight
    b. Grouping the samples by 100 and using Excel's Box Cox function to track variations in weight
    c. Manually weighing each bag and using P control charts to track variations in weight
    d. Linearly plotting the weights of each bag and logging the function to track variations in weight

2. On a control chart, what percentage of observed data values assumed to follow a normal distribution should fall within the upper and lower control limits for a process to be considered in control?
    a. 50%
    b. 75.9%
    c. 99.5%
    d. 99.7%

3. Normal instances of variation caused by routine and uncontrollable practices of the workflow are referred to as which of the following?
    a. Randomization
    b. Special acts
    c. Intermittence
    d. Common causes

4. Abnormal, abrupt, and unpredictable instances of variation that result from non-routine circumstances are referred to as which of the following?
    a. Common causes
    b. Special causes
    c. Intermittence
    d. Unique regression

5. Mike is preparing a control chart to track a process. His process doesn't have defined sample sizes, and he'll need to track the process daily for approximately three full months to obtain enough observations. Which of the following tools should he use?
    a. NP chart
    b. Excel pie chart
    c. I-MR chart
    d. U chart

6. Data from U charts almost always exhibit which of the following characteristics?
    a. Right skewedness
    b. Normal distribution
    c. Inflation
    d. Statistical insignificance

7. Ashley works in a public health clinic and treats many Medicare patients. Because the clinic is reimbursed differently through Medicare insurance, she is asked to track the percentage of patients seen who have Medicare insurance to examine the clinic's revenue cycle process. What of the following tracking tools would help Ashley with this situation?
   a. Tally sheet
   b. P chart
   c. U chart
   d. X-S chart

8. Which kind of documentation may include the action step "Stop, correct, resume"?
   a. Response plan
   b. Control log
   c. Control chart
   d. Cost-benefit analysis

9. Jessi is heading a new unit of her company. The unit will be responsible for creating a hand-held communication device. One process flow that Jessi will personally oversee is packaging the device so it can be shipped without incurring damage. Jessi begins compiling a resource that explains how packaging will take place, who will be involved, what kind of tests the package will undergo, and how testing will be monitored. Which of the following is Jessi creating?
   a. User manual
   b. Prototype
   c. High-performing team culture
   d. Control plan

10. Which of the following pillars of Total Productive Maintenance (TPM) allows machine operators to gain more knowledge about and take greater ownership of their equipment?
    a. Pillar 1 - autonomous maintenance
    b. Pillar 3 – quality integration
    c. Pillar 4 – focused improvement
    d. Pillar 5 – early equipment management

11. Which of the following is a benefit of implementing a visual factory?
    a. Employees receive long, written descriptions of processes and procedures.
    b. Work stays in process for a longer amount of time.
    c. A safer workplace is created.
    d. Errors are completely removed from the process.

Answer Explanations

1. A: X-bar & R charts, like X-S charts, track variation within groups, but require a small sample size to be accurate. The Operations Supervisor could use X-bar & R charting in the event that he was unable to quickly calculate standard deviation for his X-S charts. Box Cox transformations don't make sense in this context. Manually weighing each bag would produce data sets not normally tracked using a p chart, and it would be inefficient. Logarithms wouldn't be needed in this situation, as they are typically used to transform non-linear functions.

2. D: 99.7% of observed values fall between upper and lower control limits when a process is in control. Upper and lower control limits usually indicate three standard deviation points away from the mean in a normal distribution, which includes 99.7% of all data values. The other three options here don't include enough observations.

3. D: Common causes could include human employees who inherently work differently from each other, although they follow the same set of standardized operating procedures, or normal equipment wear and tear. None of the other options are terms using to describe process variation.

4. B: Special causes include power outages, natural disasters, and unexpectedly broken equipment. Common causes include routine instances of the workflow that can cause variation. The other two options aren't terms to describe process variation.

5. C: An I-MR chart captures observations over a moving period of time, and they are best used when sample sizes are unknown and the data-collection process is time-consuming (such as requiring three months of daily tracking). NP charts track yes/no data, and U charts track probability data. Excel pie charts would provide no functionality in this context.

6. A: The data from U charts follow the Poisson distribution, and using the assumptions of this distribution, usually result in right-skewed visual depiction.

7. B: P charts are best for instances with only two possible outcomes. In this instance, Ashley would track whether a patient had Medicare insurance. She would then express this as a fraction of the total visits. A tally sheet could be used to track patients who present Medicare insurance, but wouldn't be able to track the total counts of patients who visit. A U chart and X-S chart wouldn't be useful in tracking binomial data.

8. A: This systematic approach recommends stopping the entire process, correcting the issues, and resuming operations. "Stop, correct, resume" is a thorough response that may or may not provide an immediate solution depending on how long the corrective action takes. A control log, control chart, or cost benefit analysis does not use this system.

9. D: A control plan includes process flow, team members, testing, and control chart utilization. A control plan can also include history of the process and team, statistics that will be used, how to spot variation, and other details specific to the process and team. A user manual may be part of a control plan, but it doesn't include all of the aspects listed in the example. A prototype usually refers to a physical product. High-performing team culture is a subjective term; more details about the team would be needed for this option to be relevant.

10. A: Pillar 1 – autonomous maintenance allows machine operators to gain more knowledge about and take greater ownership of their equipment. Pillar 3 focuses on the quality aspect of maintenance and preventing defects from moving down the value chain. Pillar 4 focuses on the importance of having a large number of employees involved from various disciplines in order to bring a wide range of viewpoints and experiences to the table. Finally, pillar 5 is concerned with incorporating input from the staff who will be utilizing new equipment on its design and implementation.

11. C: Implementing a visual factory results in a safer workplace by clearly identifying hazards and safe areas. When using a visual factory method, concise instructions and graphics are used in place of long, written descriptions. The use of a visual factory also enables the work progress to take less time and decreases errors, but does not necessarily remove all errors.

FREE Test Taking Tips DVD Offer

To help us better serve you, we have developed a Test Taking Tips DVD that we would like to give you for FREE. **This DVD covers world-class test taking tips that you can use to be even more successful when you are taking your test.**

All that we ask is that you email us your feedback about your study guide. Please let us know what you thought about it – whether that is good, bad or indifferent.

To get your **FREE Test Taking Tips DVD**, email freedvd@studyguideteam.com with "FREE DVD" in the subject line and the following information in the body of the email:

> a. The title of your study guide.

> b. Your product rating on a scale of 1-5, with 5 being the highest rating.

> c. Your feedback about the study guide. What did you think of it?

> d. Your full name and shipping address to send your free DVD.

If you have any questions or concerns, please don't hesitate to contact us at freedvd@studyguideteam.com.

Thanks again!

CPSIA information can be obtained
at www.ICGtesting.com
Printed in the USA
LVHW061612240719
625191LV00010B/333/P